Sweet SPOT

How to Find Your
Private Practice Groove
with Principles from ACT

BRENDA M. BOMGARDNER

**Sweet Spot: How to Find Your Private Practice
Groove with Principles from ACT**
Published by Noetic Publishing House
Denver, CO

Publisher's Cataloging-in-Publication data

Names: Bomgardner, Brenda M., author.
Title: Sweet spot : how to find your private practice groove with principles from ACT / by Brenda M. Bomgardner.
Description: First trade paperback original edition. | Denver [Colorado] : Noetic Publishing House, 2021. | Also published as an ebook.
Identifiers: ISBN 978-0-692-11434-6
Subjects: LCSH: Small business—Management. | Psychologists—Practice.
BISAC: PSYCHOLOGY / Practice Management.
Classification: LCC HD30.28 | DDC 658 BOMGARDNER–dc22

Cover and interior design by Victoria Wolf, wolfdesignandmarketing.com

N Ö E T I C
PUBLISHING HOUSE

To all the survivors in the world who are a living testament to
the amazing resilience of the human spirit.

When the therapist is aware that he or she is in service to the soul—and this attitude does not need to be spoken—the therapy room becomes sacred space, the hour becomes sacred time, and the process becomes a ritual in the best sense of that word.

—Lionel Corbett, *The Sacred Cauldron: Psychotherapy as a Spiritual Practice*

CONTENTS

PRACTICAL KNOWLEDGE AND BUSINESS INSIGHT

LAUNCHING YOUR PRIVATE PRACTICE

INTRODUCTION

Lack of business knowledge is the single biggest factor preventing individuals with an entrepreneurial spirit from launching a private practice business and succeeding. You've completed your formal skills training and maybe you've further honed your skills by working as an employee. Where along the line did you receive adequate knowledge or training to be good at the many different aspects of running a business? Marketing, fee setting, bookkeeping, project management, revenue forecasting, and so much more can be daunting.

How do you know how to succeed at business? Failure hurts both financially and emotionally. Constant struggling week after week, month after month, and year after year to succeed hurts too. Struggling to succeed at private practice often leads to a lopsided work-life balance. Not knowing how to build your private practice can lead to working with a poor-fitting client base and early burnout, and then what?

Start over.

The attraction of believing you can simply hang out your shingle is a romantic notion that leads to unrealistic expectations of instant success. It simply does not happen. You wouldn't go on vacation without some kind of plan, so why would anyone open a private practice business without a plan?

The purpose of this book is to take your current knowledge to a whole new level of understanding. Let me tell you a story about how I know you can "level up" your knowledge base.

While working in corporate America at a Fortune 500 company as a recruiting manager and trainer in human resources, I had the opportunity to hire thousands of people over a seventeen-year period. One group of candidates I interviewed stands out as being hesitant and having doubt about their employability: women exiting the role of full-time homemaker. I frequently heard, "I don't have any work skills." In reality they had a ton of valuable transferable skills. Often they were good at budgeting, project management, creative problem-solving, and soft people skills for team building in the community.

Do you know your transferable skills? What if I told you the training you received as a therapist and healing arts professional gives you the same skills as someone with a graduate degree in business? Much of the business curricula in colleges are derived from the field of psychology. This is great news for you. It means you have the knowledge and the skills and only need a translator. That is why I wrote *Sweet Spot*.

My motivation for *Sweet Spot* is to offer you a way to translate what you already know into understandable business acumen and marketing concepts. In the deepest part of my heart and soul, I want to see people reach their highest potential and be fulfilled. To witness people leading meaningful lives, driven with a purpose that aligns with their precious dreams, is one of the greatest joys in my life and one of the core reasons I wrote this book. Along the way, I discovered that Acceptance and Commitment Therapy (ACT) is an excellent platform for enhancing the likelihood of entrepreneurial success.

Where are you now and where do you want to be? If you wait until you feel fearless and without a doubt, you might wait a very long time. Start where you are now. Feeling hesitant to move forward is a sure sign your success is important to you. Doubt motivates you to search out the best information available.

Sweet Spot will increase your psychological flexibility so you may persist or change your behavior to do what serves you best—and what works! Specifically, I want what serves you best as a private practice business owner and entrepreneur. I do this by exposing you to the six core ACT processes through dialogue and relevant exercises, including mindfulness skills, acceptance skills, and commitment to behavioral skills in taking action. I purposefully steer clear of a technical discussion on ACT. My goal is to have you experience the application of ACT to your life. To that end, I emphasize the importance of completing the exercises!

I have combined ACT with information from the emerging fields of evidence-based management and evidence-based entrepreneurship as a way to access the best available business and entrepreneurial practices. I have chosen the exercises based on studying the progress of two groups I facilitated over a two-year period. The first group ran for a year. Therapists in training explored the option of entering private practice post-graduation. The second group ran for nine months and was comprised of experienced therapists who wanted to grow their private practice. My goal was to bring the concepts, techniques, and skills grounded in ACT into the business arena as a framework for increasing entrepreneurial success. The results are reflected in this book based on the research I gathered from both groups. *Sweet Spot* is a combination of my experience as an ACT therapist, a corporate recruiter and trainer, and a private practice business owner.

I also want to help you recognize the people who are a good fit for your client base, so you can get into the groove of living a life you love both professionally and personally, which is why the exercises are also designed with practical business goals in mind. One of these practical goals is a formal business plan—the North Star to help you navigate. Throughout the book you will find references to additional exercises, which you can download from my website. These exercises include a place to start your business plan, your elevator speech and tagline, and so much more. Visit BookSweetSpot. com for the full list.

The methods you're about to read have proven results. Apply what you read in *Sweet Spot* in a wholehearted manner and you will reap the benefits. Each chapter provides an opportunity for new ways to use your current knowledge and skills in a fashion uniquely suitable to you. Let's take a quick look at ACT before you get started.

WHAT IS ACCEPTANCE AND COMMITMENT THERAPY?

The first ACT book, *Acceptance and Commitment Therapy: An Experiential Approach to Behavior Change*, was written by Steven C. Hayes, Kirk D. Strosahl, and Kelly G. Wilson in 1999. I read it in 2009 while completing my internship. What immediately fascinated me about the model, and still does, is the lack of focus on getting rid of symptoms. Rather than spending time focusing on how to cure the pains of everyday living, the focus of ACT is on living well through a process called *psychological flexibility*. The underlying six core processes contributing to psychological flexibility are embedded in *Sweet Spot*: acceptance, defusion, values clarification, committed action, self as content, and self as context.

- **Acceptance:** a willingness to hold gently or lightly your internal experience of discomfort that will show up from time to time as you navigate life.

- **Defusion:** an ability to stand back and create an internal space between you and your thoughts, feelings, sensations, urges, or other internal experiences quite often labeled as unwanted, uncomfortable, or undesirable. You will learn about defusion techniques so you can make effective choices. Defusion is not about how to get rid of or fix your thoughts or discomfort; rather, you are better able to turn toward and engage in behaviors in connection to your values.

- **Values clarification:** knowing what matters. Values clarification is often accomplished with structured exercises that facilitate a deeper understanding of the self.

- **Committed action:** doing what it takes to move toward what matters; bringing your values into fruition as a way of living a purposeful, meaningful self-directed life.

- **Self as content** and **self as context** are linked: Think of the metaphor of a book. The cover of the book is *self as context*—you are the holder of the content; in other words you are the holder of your life, the story. *Self as content* is the story of your life. There is a "you" that has been you all your life with a learning history unique to you that unfolds in the process of living your life. You will have a chance to experience both *self as content* and *self as context*. (If these two concepts seem blurry, you will gain clarity through the experiential exercises in the book.)

I invite you to hang out with me as we uncover your private practice "sweet spot" and find your groove.

SECTION

ONE

Anatomy of Change

In this first section you are going to assess your readiness to change from student or employee to a small business owner of a private practice. You will find that entrepreneurship is a creative process, as you begin to define your vision and contemplate formulating a simple yet workable business plan that will act as your North Star on your entrepreneurial journey. Along the way to clarifying your dreams you may encounter roadblocks. Some will be external, and others will appear in the form of thoughts or feelings of self-doubt, anxiety, fear, or ambivalence. I assure you the internal and external roadblocks you encounter are part of the journey. The uneasiness that turns up and the arrival of a lack of confidence belong to the territory of the entrepreneurial endeavor. You can do this.

In this first section are exercises that include concepts taken from ACT, Motivational Interviewing, and the Small Business Administration. I have sprinkled in some of my story as well as a few stories from others. Keep in mind you will have your own unique story as you travel into the world of entrepreneurship. If you discover your preference is to take a different path and not pursue private practice, this section will illuminate a path that is useful and in alignment with your heart's calling.

CHAPTER

1

How Do I Know I Am Ready?

Before opening a private practice or, as far as that goes, any small business, it is useful to take an honest look at some basic questions all entrepreneurs need to answer. Below are a few questions I have gathered along the way, which I call the Entrepreneurial Readiness Inventory.

Be honest with yourself. Answering honestly will save you a lot of heartache and money down the road. Being achievement- and success-oriented are helpful entrepreneurial traits, but it is necessary to take a 30,000-foot view of the whole process from the beginning. The questions are meant for you to start thinking about your strengths and weaknesses in regard to your time, money, and energy from this perspective.

When I was running my first twelve-month coaching group, a member I'll call Sara came to the group uncertain as to what the next step on her career path should be. The benefits of realistically taking the Inventory can be seen in Sara's story.

HONESTY IS THE BEST POLICY

Sara was an intern. Her husband was in graduate school as well and would graduate a year after she did. They had a teenage daughter at home.

Private practice deeply appealed to Sara—it was her dream! Working at an agency did not appeal to her. I enjoyed working with Sara as I watched her stick with the commitment of honestly assessing where she was in the present and where she would be in a year. She was committed to understanding the impact that being a business owner would have on the entire family. After much soul-searching, Sara decided to open her private practice after her husband finished his graduate program. She wanted to be in a place financially and energetically to devote herself to creating a private practice successfully.

Although Sara postponed opening a private practice, she found clarity about her passion, which helped her focus her job search. Clarity is beneficial regardless of whether you decide to go into private practice, defer it for later, or decide this choice is not for you. Clarity still leads you to your calling. In the coaching process, Sara created a vision and a mission statement for her private practice that ended up facilitating a focused job search: "I aim to help people suffering from the effects of abuse, trauma, and grief to heal and to live with more self-compassion, connection to others, and reliance on their inner wisdom." Furthermore, she planned "to achieve my vision by providing group and individual counseling that focuses on authenticity, compassion, balance, and creativity. I envision a counseling practice in which my clients come to embrace themselves and all of their emotions with acceptance while empowering change."

I hear she had a great interview and landed a job that would strategically prepare her for the next step into private practice. Plus, when she does open a private practice, she has completed the first step in creating a business plan.

The plan is here to help you develop a cohesive philosophy that resonates with your ideal client and others in your community. You can complete the business plan piece by piece as we go along—download the worksheet from my website. Go ahead and take peek—the plan is pretty simple.

Let's do a short present-moment exercise, then get on with the Entrepreneurial Readiness Inventory.

Present-Moment Exercise

Close your eyes for a few moments (about twenty to forty seconds) to bring yourself in contact with the present moment. Take a few breaths while you bring your attention to the tip of your nose. Notice the temperature and direction of the air as it enters and exits through your nostrils. Take about twenty breaths. OK, are you ready to read on? Feel free to make a few notes in your journal.

Entrepreneurial Readiness Inventory

As you read each question in the Entrepreneurial Readiness Inventory below, take your time. Notice if you feel excited or anxious. Being a small business owner is a lifestyle choice and feels much like jumping out of an airplane, free-falling, and hoping you packed your parachute so it will open. You may mark your answers in this book, or on a separate sheet of paper.

Some of the questions below ask you to consider your needs and wants. If your business cannot satisfy your needs and wants, chances are you will be an unhappy business owner. The Small Business Administration notes unhappiness as one of the leading causes of business failure.

1. I think I am ready to start a private practice: yes____no____

2. I have the support of family and friends for starting a private practice: yes____no____

3. I am comfortable with uncertainty, even if it means not being guaranteed a regular paycheck: yes____no____

4. I want to be my own boss and like taking charge: yes____no____

5. I want to be in charge of my financial destiny: yes____no____

6. I like to leave my work at the office at the end of the day. I think about it only when I return the next day: yes____no____

7. I am willing, and able, to concentrate on the business to the exclusion of family and friends: yes____no_____

8. I want to work____hours per day, ____hours per week.

9. I like to spend_____hours per week engaged in my hobbies or other leisure time activities.

10. I must make $_____ per year to meet my financial responsibilities.

11. I want to make $_____ per year the first year, $_____the second year, and _____by the end of five years.

12. I am in good health and have the time and energy to devote to launching a private practice: yes_____no_____

13. I am able to make decisions early, based instinctively on my own judgment, and without having complete information: yes___no___

14. I enjoy taking risks: yes___no___

15. I consider myself well organized: yes _____no_____

16. I am effective at time management: yes_____no_____

17. I am capable of seeing the big picture and all the small pieces that fit in the puzzle: yes___no___

18. I am a self-starter and like to see projects finished to the end: yes___no_____

19. People describe me as being a hard worker: yes___no___

20. I am able to take criticism and rejection and bounce back with a positive attitude: yes___no___

21. I am a creative problem solver: yes_____no_____

22. I am willing to invest money to start my private practice business: yes___no___ Amount: $_____

23. I am prepared to use some of my personal savings to start a private practice: yes____no____

24. I enjoy competition: yes____no____

25. I plan ahead: yes____ no____

SCORING

Each "YES" is worth 1 point, with the exceptions of questions 6, 8, and 9, where "NO" is worth 1 point. The higher the score, the more ready you are likely to be. You judge for yourself.

Rarely does someone answer all the questions in the Inventory with 100 percent certainty. I have seldom heard someone say they were ready, without a doubt that opening a small private practice business was exactly what they wanted to do. Even people who have been in private practice who want to take their business to the next level feel apprehensive and ambivalent. Both, apprehensions and ambivalence, are a part of the change cycle.[1] So if you are feeling a little unsure, that's normal. A little uncertainty will help you take the necessary steps and do the research needed to make choices in alignment with your dreams. You already know opening a business involves risk. And anytime we have risk and change, we humans feel uncomfortable. It is our hardwired nature to keep us safe from risk. So the real question is, are you up to it?

Ask yourself, *Am I willing and able to take the chance at succeeding in a business of my dreams?*

PERCOLATION

One attitude I advocate for everyone considering private practice is creative exploration—give yourself permission to daydream, as this holds the door open to your imagination. Percolation is an attitude of trust; your imagination is at work. The imagination is most effective when judgment is set to the side. Let your mind explore possibilities. Let it be creative in the process.

As you give yourself permission to engage in creative exploration and to percolate, you incubate your ideas—nurture them until they are ready to blossom. If you find yourself literally sitting at the kitchen table with a cup of coffee staring out the window—cool! If you get an idea, jot it down. I suggest you carry a small pad and paper or use your smartphone for those eureka moments that come into your mind in an almost mystical manner. You can record your eureka ideas as notes or as a voice memo, or even call yourself and leave a message. Capture the brilliance as it occurs.

Most of all, remain playful. Be curious like a child, with wonderment rather than judgment. If an idea or picture seems particularly sticky, take time to observe it from different perspectives. Have you heard the tale of the Six Blind Men and the Elephant?

Contextual Perspective Taking

SIX BLIND MEN AND THE ELEPHANT—
AN ANCIENT BUDDHA PARABLE

Once upon a time there lived six blind men in a village. One day the other villagers told them, "Hey, there is an elephant in the village today." The six blind men had no idea what an elephant was. They decided, "Even though we would not be able to see it, let us go and feel it anyway."

All of them went where the elephant was. Every one of them touched the elephant.

"Hey, the elephant is a pillar," said the first man, who touched his leg.

"Oh, no! It is like a rope," said the second man, who touched the tail.

"Oh, no! It is like a thick branch of a tree," said the third man, who touched the trunk of the elephant.

"It is like a big hand fan," said the fourth man, who touched the ear of the elephant.

"It is like a huge wall," said the fifth man, who touched the belly of the elephant.

"It is like a solid pipe," said the sixth man, who touched the tusk of the elephant.

Remember entrepreneurship is a creative endeavor. Exercise a flexible perspective of how private practice might look for you in your life now and how private practice might look for you in the long run. Be watchful of prescribed descriptions of what private practice is *supposed* to look like. If you find yourself talking in *shoulds*, take a break. Let your imagination run wild with possibilities.

SUMMARY

Do you think of yourself as an entrepreneur? Was your Entrepreneurial Readiness score low? I propose this thought: You made it through graduate school; you have the makings of an entrepreneur. *How so?* you ask. For one, I know you are persistent and most likely tenacious. I'll bet you even did some percolating in graduate school, most likely as part of pondering ideas in your learning process as you distilled information into useful data. Now let us turn our attention to persistence and tenacity to take a look at how each can work to help you succeed.

CHAPTER

2

Persistence, Tenacity, and

SMARTER GROWTH

Two sides of one sword named **Persistence** have a direct connection to entrepreneurial success or failure. One side cuts through discouragement, ambivalence, fear, and feelings of insecurity, providing you with a focus on achieving goals—much the same way that persistence helped you get through graduate school as you kept going back to the books. The dark side of persistence is in *not* knowing when to quit. When I say not knowing when to quit, I am referring to banging your head against the wall and bleeding to death. It is time to stop persisting when something is simply not working. Stop. Step back. Regroup.

Obviously, the bright side of persistence is the ability to stick with it. Stick with pursuing your dream. Stick with your vision, mission, and business plan. You know from past behaviors and habits that some things work, such as studying, so you repeat the study behavior until you have mastered the information. Private practice takes a degree of coming back to the same tasks and behaviors because you know they work. You also know your abilities, so if you don't have an aptitude or desire for math, for example, pursuing a graduate degree in mathematics is not in your best interest.

Tenacity is similar to persistence but makes room for trying different ways to accomplish mastery. You know sticking with studying works but only reading the material doesn't cut it. Maybe you need to take notes or make an outline, or study with another person so you can verbally learn the information. The objective of both persistence and tenacity is to find what works.

I want to stress the importance of knowing when to quit. As a rule of thumb, when persistence continues to deplete your resources, it may be time to quit. Resources can be emotional, physical, or financial. If you feel you're pounding your head on the wall and you're bleeding, stop. Therein lies the creative quality of entrepreneurship. You are the one who gets to decide what works.

Let's look at this from within the framework of ACT. ACT aims to help you create psychological flexibility, so you can get unstuck, deal with stress, and improve your well-being, which is intertwined with your private practice. If we translate psychological flexibility from the therapy world into the business world, we have **business agility**. Business agility refers to distinct qualities that allow you to respond effectively to the internal and external environment without losing your momentum or your vision.

IS IT WORKING? BE FLEXIBLE AND AGILE

Your internal environment, generally speaking, is the mind, and it presses you for the need to be agile as a therapist and entrepreneur. Your ability to expand within yourself and make room to successfully hold the nagging doubts that come with being a business owner while tenaciously pursuing your goal will take you through the bumpy spots.

I can remember when I offered my first workshop and only one person came. I had self-doubt. I wondered if I knew what I was doing. My mind has a habit of telling me I made a mistake. I experienced fear and anxiety. The fear and anxiety undermined my self-confidence. Regardless, I conducted the workshop with one person for the purpose of holding true to my intention. I did not give up; I persisted and offered another workshop. This time four people attended.

Business agility means you learn to adapt. I had to adapt. To this day I embrace the attitude of a curious scientist. The curious scientist searches for answers to one of the most significant questions in all aspects of my life: *Is it working?*

For example, a person in one of my coaching groups, who didn't like to network because she said she was too shy, decided to make cold calls. Cold calls are what telemarketers do. Need I say more? The coachee's results from cold calling were dismal, yet she was unwilling to give it up. She was persistent…without asking herself the question, *Is it working?* She could have considered her approach from the perspective of the curious scientist and spared herself a lot of time and possibly frustration. She did not, and, consequently, it took her a long time to turn her focus of time and energy toward more effective methods of networking.

I persisted in marketing my workshops in the service of growing my business and providing a service to others. I also vowed to learn more effective marketing tools. So even though uncertainty can trigger fear and anxiety, you can still persist in actions that help you grow your business and serve people.

How do you determine if something is working? In business terms it is called return on investment or ROI. You want to become aware of how you spend your time and money (resources) and see if the results warrant continued action. Without going into a complicated formula, know that ROI is an essential concept to keep in mind. Are the end results of your efforts and investment of money giving you the outcomes you desire? In the business world, ROI directly affects profitability. By the way—profit is not a bad word. Profit is the vehicle that allows you to deliver your services and satisfy your calling to serve people in a way that is meaningful and fulfilling to you. It is entirely up to you to decide what kind of vehicle (business model) you want to drive—economy, luxury, or fuel-efficient.

KNOW YOUR STRENGTHS

The results from the Entrepreneurial Readiness Inventory you took in Chapter 1 suggest two factors are helpful in entrepreneurial start-ups. One is technical preparedness, the other, psychological preparedness. Technical is not about computers. Technical in this situation is referring to the skills you need to do the job. You have the technical skills by way of your training; you are trained in counseling and/or coaching. However, you might lack business technical skills. You can join groups and get training at your local Small Business Administration center to learn about the business technical skills. Reading this book will help with the technical business skills. What about psychological preparedness? How do you hold your inner state of aversive thought patterns? In one word—lightly. Being a small business owner is hard work and being ready for the long haul is important.

A few character traits are worth mentioning as assets. How's your sense of humor? Can you laugh at yourself and not take yourself too seriously? Being able to keep your humor is necessary to help ward off burnout. Another helpful character trait is your willingness to embrace change and new ideas. All industries experience change, and your willingness to stay updated means you will thrive and not become a dinosaur. People who are slow to adjust to the essential clues in the arena of their marketplace will struggle with being relevant to their potential customers. One of the keys to thriving is being flexible. The flexibility I am referencing is the same as business agility, and it is key to a thriving private practice. Furthermore, it goes hand in hand with wise persistence and devoted tenacity.

Ineffective persistence comes into play when you devote yourself to shoring up your weaknesses. I have to admit I am not the most tech-savvy person. I consider myself a digital immigrant. It is foolish of me to think I can be as good at developing my own website as somebody who is a web developer or even somebody who is a digital native. Another weakness of mine is that I can't stand bookkeeping. What do I do about these weaknesses?

This is what I find works: I find good people with talent and character to perform the tasks I either don't like to perform or that I am not good at performing. (More on this in Chapter 15.)

It's important you spend your time wisely. You don't need to get better at your weaknesses; you need to get better at your strengths. Your strength is your calling, whether it is massage therapy or talk therapy or coaching. Why get better at your strengths? Because that's how you develop expertise in your chosen niche and that will set you apart from the crowd. And this translates into a marketing advantage. Peter Drucker firmly asserts, "One should waste as little effort as possible on improving areas of low competence. It takes far more energy and work to improve from incompetence to mediocrity than it takes to improve from first-rate performance to excellence."[2] It can also be expensive.

New private practice owners, even with tons of therapy experience, distract themselves with more and more training in areas that don't necessarily fit their niche or their passions. People do this in an effort to get rid of the unwelcome feelings of discomfort associated with fear. One thing I hear from my coaching clients is, "I don't feel confident, and I feel like an imposter." It is also human nature to move away from discomfort; technically this is called *experiential avoidance*. The truth of the matter is you suck at a lot of stuff. The good thing is we all suck at a lot of stuff, and that's OK. Work on improving what you are already good at and passionate about.

Next I want to introduce you to a couple of tools that have been proven to help with motivation and goal achievement. SMARTER GROWTH analysis can help if you struggle with what I mentioned earlier—persistence and tenacity with what works. As I introduce these tools, keep in mind that agility is the hallmark of resilience. Sometimes when using goal-setting tools, a person can become overly fixated on accomplishing the goal and lose sight of other significant clues in the environment. Rigid goal-setting can lead to a narrowing of vision—tunnel vision. My advice about tools: hold them lightly so you do not let them narrow your awareness skills. Being aware and mindful are vital to prudent decisions and business agility.

SMARTER GROWTH **TOOLS**

Edwin A. Locke, an organizational psychologist, was a pioneer in goal-setting theory and helped originate the development of SMART goals in the mid-1980s along with Gary P. Latham, professor of organizational effectiveness. The acronym SMART, which I explain later in this chapter, is used as a tool for goal achievement, organizational success, job satisfaction, and personal growth. The "ER" was added after Locke and Latham developed the SMART model.[3]

Also in the mid-'80s, the GROW model of executive coaching was developed by the pioneering work of Sir John Whitmore, Graham Alexander, and Alan Fine.[4] The GROW method taps into problem-solving skills with the purpose of enhancing employee performance and development. Research by Peter Gollwitzer, professor of psychology at New York University, led to the addition of "TH" to the model in the early 1990s. GROWTH brings into focus the transformational aspect of goal achievement. As Zig Ziglar says, "What you get by reaching your goals is not nearly as important as what you become by reaching them."[5] The pursuit of a goal changes who you are.

The *becoming* aspect of striving for your goals, and living in alignment with what matters most to you, most likely sounds familiar, as this is what we hope for and dream of for our clients. The GROWTH model shields us from adverse negative inner states by focusing on the when, where, and how of goal achievement.

By connecting the two models of SMARTER and GROWTH and translating them into the ACT model, we end up touching on the six core processes of ACT. SMARTER GROWTH distinctly encourages clarity of values and willingness to take committed action even while facing uncomfortable and often unwanted feelings of fear and insecurity. Willingness is the acceptance piece of ACT. SMARTER GROWTH also encourages defusion by asking for a realistic assessment. You need to step back to look objectively where you are and where you want to go. Plus, this is done in the present moment while stepping outside the static role of the conceptualized self. When we take the risk to pursue something important, we often encounter some form of fear. Anxiety, worry, apprehension, insecurity, ambivalence, overwhelm, and confusion, to name a few, are grounded in fear. The tendency for our inner states to derail us are calmed with intentional focus on pragmatic steps. Both SMARTER and GROWTH are evidence-based coaching models to help us move forward. I have paired SMARTER with GROWTH into a single model. This formula acts as a motivator in long-term goal realization and self-coaching success.

How does SMARTER GROWTH support persistence and tenacity in the process of change? The transition from employee or student to private practice business owner is a move from what you know to the unknown. SMARTER GROWTH is a tool to develop a pragmatic plan of action toward your desire for a fulfilling future. It acts like a roadmap. It helps you leverage your persistence and tenacity. With SMARTER GROWTH you are equipped for the journey.

The *Sweet* SPOT
Success Model

Figure 1: Sweet Spot Success Model

Now it is time to take a look at the model and how the components relate to each other. The model will answer three major questions:

- Are my goals well-defined?

- Do I have the right strategies?

- Can I execute the strategies?

First, what are the words inside each acronym? SMART is how you operationalize your goal. Goals are: (S) Specific, (M) Meaningful, (A) Adaptive, (R) Relevant, and (T) Time Bound. I fit SMART inside of GROWTH, which stands for: (G) Goals, (R) Reality, (O) Obstacles and Options, (W) Willingness, (T) Tactics, and (H) Habits. The "ER" at the end of SMART is discussed separately as a next level in the evolution of goal theory.

Details of SMARTER GROWTH

Goals: What do you want to accomplish? Take a moment to see if you can clearly state what it is you want to work toward. The idea is to describe a goal that will be obvious to you when you have accomplished it. Well-defined goals meet the following criteria:

- **Specific**: A goal needs to contain details of what the end results will look like. It can be broken down into a step-by-step process of attainment. Example: My goal is to have a thriving private practice. I want to see six clients per day, three days a week, and work from 9 a.m. to 3 p.m., and make enough money ($60,000) to pay my bills; the other two days I will perform administrative duties and network for professional and personal growth. Example: I want to launch my full-time private practice in the historical old town area, working with women who struggle with anxiety and depression.

- **Meaningful**: Is your goal connected to your values? In the traditional SMART model the "M" is normally ascribed as "measurable." However, just because a behavior can be measured does not mean it has any significance in a person's life. For example, a rowing team that can be measured at a fast rowing speed means nothing if the rowing is taking the team into a sandbar and not the finish line. That's why it is important you occasionally check in with yourself to see if what you are doing is connected to a goal that is meaningful. Other private practice entrepreneurs might have strong opinions about what constitutes a meaningful goal. Be cautious and hold true to your unique vision and mission. An added byproduct of goals being connected to meaningful values is nourishment for motivation. It is much easier to do the *hard* work if you know what it means to you. People I have worked with have told me that having a thriving private practice and earning a sustainable wage have allowed them to spend more time with loved ones and to travel. Others have said that owning a private practice allows them to have greater creative freedom in helping people transcend their suffering and heal.

- **A**daptable: Does your goal set you up for a life that works? The standard SMART acronym used "A" for "achievable." Being able to achieve something without meaning holds little pizzazz. "Adaptable" is a more ACT-consistent stance. Does your goal improve your ability to flexibly live your life in a meaningful and fulfilling manner? Does this goal or behavior move you toward what is important to you? Thus, the call is for you to become clear about your overarching values in your professional and personal life. In my life, having a private practice meets an overarching value of learning, which includes professional development and leadership in the counseling and coaching industry. Maintaining a private practice allows me freedom, which allows me time to write. As you can see, adaptability refers to a good fit in your life.

- **Relevant**: Does your goal actually matter to you? Make sure your goal drives you toward something worthwhile to you. Can you articulate what is worthwhile about your goal? Does it match who you want to be in the world? Is the timing right for where you are in the world right now? Review your answers to the Entrepreneurial Readiness Inventory. Would it be better to wait? Use your wisdom. Wisdom comes in many forms, and it takes an attentive ear to hear it. Listen to yourself.

- **Time Bound**: Set a date for starting and completing. Example: I will begin to write a business plan on the first of the month and finish it by the end of the month. Example: I will identify an office building for the location of my private practice by the middle of the month, and then I will call the property manager to set up an appointment within one week after I have identified a property. This is time management and a must for all entrepreneurs. If there is no deadline, there is little chance to adjust your plans on your journey. A word of caution: Be flexible. If you miss a deadline, this does not translate into failure. It means you need to develop a new plan or revise your plan. It means you need to *adjust* something.

- **Evaluate**: Assess whether your original goal needs to be adjusted. Ask yourself, "Does this goal excite me?" *Exciting* may include feelings of fear and anxiety, which are normal. Exciting points toward things that are important to you. Do you feel empowered by your goal to take action? Are you inspired to persevere?

- **Revise** your goal. This last step is so you are not locked into an unworkable goal or one that doesn't fit. It's a step you can only take after you begin. This allows for flexibility.

Reality: Where are you now? Take stock of what you already have in your favor. What do you need to begin your journey? Do you already have ideas about who you want to work with or where you want to set up your office? As a coaching assignment, I ask people to write out nine simple goals they want to accomplish in ninety days to get the ball rolling. What are your nine goals? What is the likelihood you are ready to accomplish those nine goals? If you're not ready, create smaller goals. Stop reading after you finish this sentence and take time to write down the nine simple goals you want to accomplish over the next ninety days on the worksheet you can download from my website. This is important! See if your nine goals fit into the SMARTER GROWTH format. If not, no worries. They will continue to develop and evolve as you continue to read.

Obstacles and Options: As you assessed the reality of where you are with your goals, did you come across any obstacles? Are some of your obstacles internal? Most of us have internal yucky stuff that gets in the way. As Gollwitzer discovered, the inner states that feel aversive can derail us from pursuing our goals. ACT gives us options on how to relate to these inner obstacles with a method called **defusion**. Defusion is the ability to observe problematic thoughts and feelings from a distance, allowing us to become untangled or disconnected from their literal meaning. You will have opportunities to experience defusion techniques throughout this book. Right now all you need to know are the basic steps of stop, step back, and observe in the present moment.

The "O" also stands for **options**, which are actually **opportunities**. When you come right down to it, every obstacle brings with it an opportunity to learn or create something new. The inner state of fear, anxiety, and worry is part of the journey and can't actually be solved as a problem. We can learn to take a stance of expansion. To be big enough to hold lightly the yucky stuff that shows up and persist toward our goals. It is similar to working with clients and being open to the creative process of therapy and coaching.

Willingness: Willingness is your ability to commit to taking action and being open to what shows up. I want to touch on the idea of marketing your private practice business. Often I hear therapists and healers say they don't like to market. The words I hear are, "I want a thriving private practice with 'my' kind of clients, but marketing feels slimy, fake, and manipulative. I don't want to 'SELL' myself!!" Connect back to your values and use defusion skills. Willingness is the ability to persist when doing so will move you forward toward your goals. Defusion and willingness pave the way to success.

Tactics: What are some of the tactics you have used in the past that might work now? Within ACT, the tactics that work are finding clarity about your values, opening up to what shows up, then doing what matters. Beyond the ACT model, more specifically: what is your plan, what are your policies, and what is your line of attack?

Habits: What routine will help? It is harder to break a bad habit than it is to create a new habit. Putting a routine in place from the beginning is best practice. I got some good advice from my friend Tamara Suttle when she told me to go to the office every day and maintain regular hours even if I did not have a single client. I am passing this advice on to you. Create a work routine. Start a group and meet once a week to hold each other accountable. Do something on a regular basis that moves you toward your dream. If nothing else, take this book with you to the office every day and work on clarifying your sweet spot, business plan, or marketing plan. Use the **SMARTER GROWTH** worksheets (Nine Goals in 90 Days) from BookSweetSpot. com, and work on your goals and time management.

The Tactics and Habits added to GROW are an *if-then* formula for behavior modification. For instance: *If* I get nervous before a networking event, I will *then* rehearse my elevator speech out loud. *If* I rehearse my elevator speech, I will *then* be better prepared for networking. In the realm of behavior modification, *if-then* helps automate behaviors for greater success at goal attainment. Many of us set out to reach a goal and then refrain from engaging in behaviors toward goal attainment or we fail to follow through. What amazes me about all this business talk is that it is grounded in the field of psychology. The broader your understanding of therapy processes, the better you are at understanding business processes and vice versa.

BE SMARTER

You can take SMART to the next level and develop **SMARTER** goals. Can you believe it? SMART with ER creates an opportunity for you to be agile. "E" is for "evaluate." Take time to assess your goals, your obstacles, your actions, and your successes. "R" is "revise." This is delicate, as sometimes our mind will tell us one thing about failure, but what might be needed is persistence. Revision is a judgment call. Evaluating and revising are ongoing processes that can temper the narrow and rigid pursuit of a goal.

SMARTER GROWTH leads to ongoing committed actions, clarity of goals attached to values, and sustained energy. An added benefit is that the model exhibits compatibility with many therapeutic frameworks. Therefore, a practitioner can utilize it with clients.

Here is a little secret that can help with goal setting and goal achievement: write your goal down and share it verbally with a trusted individual. The success rate of accomplishing a goal is greatly increased by sharing. Verbal sharing increases your persistence and tenacity in the creative process of change and entrepreneurship. The icing on the cake is how you feel once you have accomplished your goal. People who verbally share their goals experience a bigger sense of accomplishment. When you are sharing your goals, share your intentional plan on how to step-by-step accomplish them. Go ahead and share your Nine Goals in 90 Days.

SMARTER GROWTH *Exercise*

Let's practice. Use the worksheet Nine Goals in 90 Days (downloaded from my website) to create a brief summary of your goal(s). This will make remembering and focusing easier. Keep in mind as you look at your completed worksheets that you can fill out the below list in any order. Hint: sometimes it's best to start with Reality, then see what comes up next. You might find there is an overlap in the information. Pick one of your goals from the worksheet and begin. You can use a separate sheet of paper, or write in your journal. Keep it simple and keep it brief.

- What is your **Goal**?
  - State it: Be ***Specific*** (and concise).
  - In what way is it ***Meaningful*** to you?
  - How does it help you ***Adapt*** to better live your life?
  - Is it ***Relevant*** to what is important to you?
  - ***Time Bound*** to what date?
  - ***Evaluate*** progress and
    - ***Revise*** and tweak your goal. (Pick a time to the beginning of setting a goal to ***Evaluate*** and ***Revise*** and mark your calender)
- What's your current **Reality**?
- What **Obstacles** and **Options** are present?
- Do you posses the **W**illingness to go for it?
- What **T**actics will you employ?
- Do you need new **H**abits?

Modify the tool so that it is useful to you. Remain agile. Visit SweetSpot. com for a worksheet.

SUMMARY

I have touched on a few behavioral characteristics of persistence, tenacity, and flexibility (business agility), which are helpful in successfully navigating entrepreneurship. We have taken a peek at business terms and business tools, all in the service of discovering what works for you and your business. I will continue to flesh out the business terms as transferable skills you already possess as a well-trained therapist. In the next chapter, we will look at how gatekeepers and private practice myths prey on fears and act as barriers to entering private practice.

3

Don't Let the Gatekeepers Shut the Door on Your Dreams

You've begun to examine your readiness to enter private practice. You have a couple of self-coaching tools—the Entrepreneurial Readiness Inventory and SMARTER GROWTH exercise—to help you stay focused. In the process of pursuing your calling you will come across gatekeepers and myths. We are going to take a look at both and shine a light on the function of each.

But first I want to talk about your childhood. Do you remember being afraid of the dark? How about believing in Santa Claus or the tooth fairy? You have grown up and your beliefs have changed. You have learned new ways of understanding the world. Your body has changed too. You have gained new skills such as riding a bike and driving a car. Relationships have come and gone.

The cool thing about looking back toward childhood and your younger self is that you can be here now and know what it was like there and then as a child. You experience perspective. Perspective-taking allows you to hold stories lightly. You no longer let myths guide your behavior.

MYTHS

I want to demystify some misleading beliefs about private practice. In order to do this, a little history is called for.

Myths and folklore have been around since the time of the Greek gods and goddesses. According to anthropologist William R. Bascom, myths and folklore exist to apply social pressure on and gain conformity from individuals and groups and justify the rituals of the ruling class. Myths are a pedagogic device that reinforce the morals and values of the powerful. Generally speaking, people in power want to stay in power.

Gatekeepers defend the powerful by sharing commonly held beliefs—in this case, myths about the path into private practice. Don't believe everything you hear. I was naïve and learned this the hard way.

As a new practitioner, I felt insecure and sought wisdom from the tribe of experienced private practice business owners, the elders. I had a naïve belief that the elders, who are professional helpers, would want to help me succeed. I soon discovered this was an illusion. It was painfully apparent the system was organized to keep a hierarchal structure in place. The helping culture is a microcosm of the rest of Western civilization's business culture, which is competitive and territorial. I realized I needed to push past the myths and folklore perpetuated by the gatekeepers if I wanted to succeed.

I heard the following statements when I was launching my business, and to this day I still hear the words of a few of the gatekeepers rumbling in my head when I "toot my own horn" about a new project or endeavor. If you have heard any of these statements, you may well agree the tone of voice often rings a dire warning. I encourage you to exercise a mindful noticing as you read.

- "You need to work at an agency for at least two or more years before going out on your own." (Translated: you owe it to the community to martyr yourself and sacrifice.)

- "If you haven't worked at an agency, you really don't know how to do real therapy with the real problems people have." (Translated: there is only one way to be qualified and that is my way, and I regret I had to work for next to nothing.)

- "You have to pay your dues." (Translated: go do agency work.)

- "If you talk too much about your success in your business, people won't like you, then they won't refer you." (Translated: professional jealousy.)

- "Don't develop a brand focused on your niche because we don't refer to a brand, we refer to people because this is a people business." (Translated: the folklore of olden days—keeping the status quo and keeping you in your place.)

- "There are too many people already doing what you want to do, and the competition is too much to make a go of it. Stop before you lose your shirt." (Translated: stay put and stay stuck.)

- "You're not really qualified until you _____ [fill in the blank]."

- "You have to work 10,000 hours before you're really good at what you do. Hence, you better wait to hang your shingle."

The underlying message is *Keep out! No trespassing! No admission! Private practice is sacred.* Consequently, since the job of the mind is to keep you safe, you may find yourself getting hooked by these messages—roadblocks put before you by the gatekeepers.

The last comment in the list is from Malcom Gladwell's book, *Outliers: The Story of Success*. Gladwell's message is you can only become an expert and proficient at a skill if you have 10,000 hours of practice under your belt. This translates into a decade. There is some debate centered on Gladwell's claim. According to Daniel Goleman in his book *Focus: The Hidden Driver of Excellence*, purposeful attention and focus are the factors that lead to high performance and fulfillment. Goleman's research on smart practices for mastery points to skills such as mindfulness meditation, focused preparation and recovery (corrective action), positive emotions, and connections leading to improved habits, skills, and sustainability. He puts these skills into three attentional mental categories: inner, other, and outer. These are behaviors you most likely already practice; hence, I am saying to you, you have what it takes to succeed in private practice regardless of what the gatekeepers tell you.

I am not saying everybody is competitive and territorial. I am saying you need to pay attention and notice. Look for people who are collaborative, supportive, and open to new ideas. You can expect to use the same skills to thrive in the business world of private practice as you would in any competitive situation. Notice your answers to the following questions:

- How did you get into to graduate school?

- How did you find an internship site?

- How did you get a job earning money before or during grad school?

Do you see you possess the necessary skills to succeed? Do you understand your ability to persist at behaviors important to you to achieve your goals? Persistence, or what Paula Andruss, a writer for *Entrepreneur*, calls dedication or drive, is one of the top five traits you need to dominate in your industry. Maybe you did not realize it at the time, but you successfully competed for a limited opportunity at grad school, employment, and an internship. It is in your nature to be driven when it comes to something important to you as you have a proven track record with the investment of your time, energy, and resources.

Let's examine Goleman's three categories.

INNER, OTHER, AND OUTER SKILLS

"Inner" focus taps into your therapeutic skill of being able to pay attention and notice your own thoughts, feelings, and sensations in the process with a client. Put another way, inner focus is self-awareness in the present moment while being able to keep your eye trained on long-term goals. This type of self-awareness leads to stellar performance in the form of emotional self-control and the ability to quickly recover from distressing feelings. In ACT terms, I equate this to acceptance and perspective-taking in the service of values-based action.

"Other" focus is being aware of the surroundings in your environment. As a therapist, other focus is the main purpose of your work, the client. However, it does not stop there. Although not talked about, some of the things we do as therapists are influencing, inspiring, and motivating our clients toward a state of well-being (based on what they define as well-being). We do this in a collaborative manner with their consent. At the heart of collaboration is empathy. I'll bet you are excellent at empathy. When inner focus and other focus are combined, we arrive at emotional intelligence. I'll bet you are great at emotional intelligence too!

"Outer" focus is the ability to see systems. Private practice lives in the system of the healing arts community. With outer focus you read how the forces of the larger community influence the marketplace and eventually your business. You are most likely aware of systems at play in the therapeutic world when working with individuals as they put forth effort to change. As a therapist, you know there is a great deal of power in place to keep the system protected.

Relating this to ACT, outer focus is the ability to take perspective from the observer position. "The skills that form 'Focus,'" according to the Greater Good Science Center, on Goleman's work, "range from staying calm under pressure and the discipline and drive to continually improve, to empathy, persuasion, and conflict management. A person's ability to harness these skills predicts who will be an outstanding leader, team member, or solo performer."[6] The word "nimble" describes how one focuses attention.

Back to gatekeepers and myths: the system is protecting itself and trying to maintain the status quo. The list of discouraging statements I received from my elders plays into our basic human fear of change and our mind's desire to be safe. Risk is dangerous.

How does your mind keep you safe? It will try to hook you into staying safe (stuck) with thoughts like:

- You're not good enough.

- You don't know enough.

- You will fail.

- It's too hard.

- It's too risky.

- You'll lose your ass.

- You can't succeed.

- There are too many therapists.

- I am afraid.

Sure, you want to make prudent decisions, and I encourage you to perform the necessary due diligence. Here's a bit of common-sense caution for you at this stage of contemplation: use scrutiny, be a little skeptical of what is being said, and consider the source (who is saying it) and what function it serves that person and the system—then apply appropriate filters. By applying common-sense caution, you will be able to answer the following relevant question: *is there any validity to their statement that may serve as helpful information to move you toward your purpose in life?*

What is the cost of giving the keys to your dreams to the naysayers in the world, including the voice of your pessimistic inner critic and the doubter in your mind?

There was a time when the system was more open. We call this The Golden Age of Therapy.

THE GOLDEN AGE OF THERAPY

You may discover a difference in attitudes among practitioners who entered the mental health field in the '70s and '80s and those who have recently entered the field. The history of mental health exerts a strong influence on perception and practice. Let's take a brief look at this over the last half-century. The goal here is to gain some perspective of how history collides with present-day beliefs and practices. Being able to do some perspective-taking allows you to be aware and open-minded to possibilities.

It is estimated that by 1970, more than 60,000 people who were considered feebleminded, imbeciles, idiots, and mentally defective were sterilized in the United States.[7] During World War II, Germany euthanized more than 300,000 people considered mentally disabled. This was a turning point in mental health history as the American public became more sensitive to the treatment of individuals suffering from some sort of mental challenge.

In 1971, the United Nations offered its Declaration on the Rights of Mentally Retarded Persons, making it official that those with a mental handicap had rights and were to be treated with dignity. Prior to this era, the President's Committee on Mental Retardation was formed (1966) followed by the founding of the Special Olympics (1968). Even earlier, in the 1950s, parents had formed the National Association for Retarded Children. Consequently, the '70s ushered in the "Golden Age" of mental healthcare with advocacy and acceptance, a collective effort to do justice for people with disabilities through case law and statutory law.

Lynn Grodzki, author and small business coach, defines the Golden Age of Therapy as an era that lasted well into the 1980s when clients (then called patients) could count on long-term therapy with excellent benefits paid for by their insurance company.[8] To start a private practice, which was viewed as an almost priestly, mysterious calling and not as a business, a practitioner "hung a shingle," bought business cards, made a few phone calls to medical doctors and trusted friends to ask for referrals, and waited for patients (clients) to start calling for appointments. Practitioners shied away from the language of promotion, marketing, self-branding, and profit maximization—activities considered ill-disposed to the sanctity of the therapeutic enterprise. It was considered in bad taste to blaze your own trail and toot your own horn about your private practice business. The Golden Age was also an easier time to enter the field and make a living. According to Grodzki, the Golden Age has been replaced by the Aluminum Age: the less precious, more utilitarian perception of therapy by the public and our profession itself. No longer seen as elite healers, therapists are now commonplace service providers of healthcare.

Fast-forward to the mid-'90s as healthcare reform occurred under President Clinton with the passing of The Health Security Act of 1994. This opened the door for managed competition calling for universal care and government regulation to control costs. The side effect brought in an *unintended* era of managed care with the focus on keeping costs down. No longer could an individual or family enter therapy knowing they would have low co-pays and unlimited visits for mental healthcare with a provider of their choice. Today, co-pays are often high and the yearly visits are limited—sometimes as few as four to six sessions depending on the mental illness diagnosis.[9]

Why does it matter? The times are changing almost daily. When I started writing *Sweet Spot*, the Affordable Care Act (ACA) was passed in March 2010 and took hold in 2014, under the leadership of then-President Barack Obama. More people were insured with access to mental healthcare than at any other time in history. Congress then took an about-face under the leadership of President Donald Trump, which began working hard at repealing the ACA legislation. A serious question comes to mind: *as a provider, can you sustain yourself with a living wage based on the reimbursement rate given by the insurance companies?* This question is important because change can be rapid, and a solid game plan will provide a stable foundation for attracting clients and building a path toward growth. It's kind of like a treatment plan for progress, except it's called a business plan (see my website to download the worksheet).

I highly encourage a business plan that includes self-pay so as not to be at the whim of legislation and under the thumb of managed care. With all the uncertainty, the bottom line is you are the only one who can make the decision about your practice based on your values and your commitment—not any of the gatekeepers. It is your responsibility and you get to live with the results of your choices. This is the same respect we give to clients. They live with the consequences of their decisions. Clarity and perspective are called for as you make important decisions for your future.

STIGMA AND MENTAL HEALTH

Although the times are changing, there are leftover myths floating around about people who go to therapy. Mental health has not escaped the stigma of mental illness. Although consumers of mental health services are more informed, they can still feel the judgment of being seen as broken or weak. A diagnosis can lead to employment discrimination (another reason to develop a business plan with self-paying clients as part of your caseload). At the most innocuous level, a person seeking therapy services is considered "stuck."

The image and identity of the mental health field are struggling against the concept of not being a valued health agenda. Even with the ACA and the 2008 Mental Health Parity Act, benefits and reimbursement rates were and still are notoriously low. As Susan Brink writes in *U.S. News*, "Provisions of the new laws…represent the latest attempts to provide preventive services and comprehensive treatment for mental health that [are] equivalent to that provided for physical health. No oncologist would say, 'You're entitled to ten treatments, and then your cancer coverage stops.' Yet that's exactly what mental health patients have heard. No cardiologist would tell a patient, 'If you relapse into high blood pressure, your treatment is considered a failure.'"[10]

Let's revisit the Golden Age of Therapy, as a few antiquated rules have stuck around from that bygone era. The elite culture of gatekeepers—almost priestly healers—is still present. However, the mental health and healing arts industry has moved closer to a marketplace where educated consumers drive the show. The educated consumer is online comparing, contrasting, and learning as they shop for mental health and wellness services. They are looking to maximize their limited resources of time and money. In general, the healthcare industry is moving away from a *client-centered* system to a *client-driven* system. This translates into the client being the expert on their wants and needs, and providers and practitioners assuming a role closer to a facilitator of process. Be cautious and don't believe everything you hear when embarking on a path toward opening a private practice business. As I mentioned earlier, even your own mind will have something to say about the risk involved with the daring jump.

SUMMARY

When gathering information to make an informed decision, it is easy to get sidetracked with the desire to analyze it all. Sometimes our minds grab onto information that feeds our fear rather than empowers us to pursue our dreams. I've highlighted a few of the possible roadblocks you may encounter in the process of identifying a course of action. Look for people who will support you in cultivating your dreams. In the next chapter we further examine the connection of choice and commitment and how they carry you through the temptation to quit.

As a side note about the Golden Age for the therapeutic field. It was not the Golden Age for people of color (POC). Minorities were and still are not the demographics as an intended population for mental health care. However, the prison system demographic is 60% blacks and Hispanics. The "priestly calling" of the golden age did not reach or include people of color. It was not Golden Age for all.

The Starting Line

M uch like running a race, you first need to make a choice that you want to enter the race then you need to prepare for the race. And there is the question of how you are going to stay motivated, what strategies you are going to use, and who can tell you how to compete in the race. There is no need to reinvent the wheel. At the same time, you make it your race. Your style and your strategies are unique to you. This section is how to get to the starting line with effective strategies. Being an entrepreneur is more like a marathon than a sprint, so you need to prepare from the very beginning. I am giving you the best information available to approach the starting line armed with long-term results in mind. As you read the next few chapters, let yourself begin to make it your race: your game and your private practice business.

CHAPTER

4

Cultivating Choice and Commitment

After taking a glance at some of the roadblocks that might derail you from your dreams, you are left with the choice of moving forward or not. Commitment is the willingness to carry out your plan. It takes doing the first steps.

Doing is the operative word here. Making a commitment and not doing is known as wishful thinking. Commitment is a way of traveling with a posture of willingness and being open to the experience of uncertainty. I think of commitment and choice as a form of gardening. Pick your spot then tend to your garden. From this point of view "shoulds" are like weeds in the garden. Cultivate the garden, not the weeds.

SHOULDS

When you find yourself uttering the word **should** in connection to a way of being, you've probably adopted an arbitrary rule from past learning. **Shoulding** (sounds a lot like sh*ting when we say it aloud) all over yourself is a sure way to end up feeling drained and oppressed. Shoulding is a stinky spot to be in, and when it comes to private practice, shoulding leads to feeling used up. The antidote is *commitment* to a value-guided way of living: an ongoing process that supports the purpose of our goals.

Choosing to make a commitment based on your values disarms the shoulding trap. The byproduct of choosing to engage in behavior in alignment with your values is a sense of aliveness. You can detect this disarmament by looking for a sense of aliveness and excitement even in the face of fear.

Gardening[11] Exercise

"Imagine that you selected a spot to plant a garden. You worked the soil, planted the seeds, and waited for them to sprout. Meanwhile, you started noticing a spot just across the road, which also looked like a good spot—maybe even a better spot. So you pulled up your vegetables and went across the street and planted another garden there. Then you noticed another spot that looked even better. Values are like the spot where you plant a garden. You can grow some things very quickly, but others require time and dedication. The question is, 'Do you want to live on lettuce, or do you want to live on something more substantial—potatoes, beets, and the like?' You can't find out how things work in gardens when you have to pull up stakes again and again. Of course, if you stay in the same spot, you'll start to notice its imperfections. Maybe the ground isn't quite as level as it looked when you started, or perhaps the water has to be carried for quite a distance. Some things you plant may seem to take forever to come up. It is at times like this that your mind will tell you, 'You should have planted elsewhere.' 'This will probably never work.' 'It was stupid of you to think you could grow anything here,' and so on. The choice to garden here allows you to water and weed and hoe, even when these thoughts and feelings show up."

What did you notice as you read? What do you hope to grow in the way of a private practice business? Perhaps you have an unspoken philosophy that needs to be articulated—a cluster of guiding principles. Take a moment and jot down a few thoughts about what's important to you, either in your journal, or using the worksheet for the business plan on my website.

These thoughts are the seeds for eventually composing a vision and mission statement (we will cover these in Chapter 10), and eventually business plan, for your private practice business. You don't need to have a clear vision, mission, or philosophy now though; you're percolating. However, take notes if something seems salient. If you feel confused and things seem cloudy, that's OK too. Then again, you may notice a strong belief percolating up to the surface in a eureka moment. If this is the case, write a line or two about your belief.

COMMITMENT

Embedded in the garden metaphor is the committed action of making a choice and sticking with that choice. As you gain clarity about what you dream your private practice business will be about, you will persist with behaviors that move you toward your goals.

This is no different than what practitioners ask of their clients. We ask clients to make a commitment to come to therapy on a regular basis. We ask them to persist. We know therapy works well when a client makes a wholehearted commitment. We work at facilitating change with our clients as they transform their relationship with suffering. We do this from a stance of flexibility. The garden will most likely flourish when, rather than transplanting, we are flexible in tending to it. You can prepare the soil, but you will need to figure out how much water, when and what to weed, and if fertilizer is needed. The balancing act is persistence tempered with flexibility at cultivating what works. You may need to do something different when what you are doing is not working. A business has a developmental cycle just as plants do—and that is what we will look at next.

STAGES IN THE BUSINESS CYCLE

I am going to borrow from a theory about small group dynamics with a focus on stages of group development and apply the theory loosely to business growth.[12] The stages are: forming, storming, norming, performing, and adjourning. You probably studied groups in your graduate program, so this will sound familiar.

Each stage has tasks to accomplish to move to the next. The task in the **forming** stage is preparation, which is what you are doing right now as you read this book. Preparing the soil, if we are using the garden metaphor. Currently you are engaged in creative exploration, gathering information, completing a business plan, and more, depending on your needs. The tasks for the **storming** stage, as I define it here, is the actual launching of your private practice business and the relationships you will form to accomplish a successful launch. You will form a team through relationships with landlords, bookkeepers, lawyers, web designers, graphic artists, colleagues, suppliers, etc. You may experience conflict along the way as you negotiate these newly formed relationships. This is expected and leads to the third stage.

Norming is when you settle in and begin to experience some stability with knowing what to expect. You form rules based on what you learned in the storming stage to govern your business life and personal life. Chances are you will gain a sense of comfortable yet quiet confidence as your private practice business becomes profitable. The tasks in the fourth stage, **performing**, include the opportunity to grow through diversifying or expanding your private practice business. The fifth and final stage is **adjourning**. Planning for the adjourning stage from the beginning can lead to a private practice business you can sell or one that has set you up for retirement. Hopefully, your long-terms goals will lead to a private practice business that has a value in the marketplace.

One of the reasons to develop a business plan is to have a roadmap for your short- and long-term future as you navigate each stage. The stages may repeat themselves to some degree as your business cycles through times of growth or change. Below is a short story about Carol in her first and second developmental stages.

Carol signed a lease, ordered business cards, and started seeing clients. She was filled with energetic eagerness. She had worked in the corporate world for years before re-careering. What stood out to me was her excitement about her business cards, which was contagious. She had had business cards before in her corporate life, but there was something intensely thrilling about her very own business card with a unique logo she had designed with the help of a graphic artist she hired. She handed out those new business cards with the pride of a new parent. It was as if she actually had a newborn baby. She talked endlessly about her adorable, newly launched business. Her passion was gleaming.

In the beginning, you may find yourself feeling like a new parent, watching over and worrying about your business. Pride, fear, and apprehension are normal for most new parents. Notice a wide range of feelings and notice your willingness to experience the wave of emotions. Ideally, take this time of excitement to make choices to help your private practice business thrive. You may find yourself in Carol's shoes, parading your new business at networking events and talking to your family, friends, neighbors, and grocery store clerks. Great! Do it! This promotes healthy growth. I encourage you to enjoy this time, because it is your new business, and this excitement and energy are exactly what a newborn business needs to take root.

Each stage of the business development cycle requires a different focus and a new commitment. *Sweet Spot* is mainly focused on the first two stages. Business-speak has its own names for the cycle. I would like to introduce you to the names of these stages in business-speak:

1. Seed and Development

2. Launch and Start-Up

3. Growth and Establishment

4. Expansion

5. Maturity and Exit

What do you think? Do you see these are similar to how we as therapists have been taught about small group development and dynamics: forming, storming, norming, performing, and adjourning?

I want to make another point. We know that a large number of businesses fail before their fifth year. Consequently, it only makes good sense to give the first two stages careful and intentional consideration. Once the second stage begins to emerge, it is essential to maintain a keen focus on agility. Looking from the perspective of small group development at stage two (storming), the launching and start-up stage, you can see it is crucial to be able to navigate the conflict between what we plan and what is reality, as well as conflict or inconsistency with members in our new community. Many of the skills you use as a therapist will come in handy at each stage throughout the life cycle of your private practice business.

It is a challenge to be prepared for something you have never done before. There is nothing I can tell you that will guarantee you a completely foolproof plan for launching a private practice business, any more than a book can totally prepare you to ride a bike. Here is the truth: It takes doing to know. Like many things in life—riding a bike, skiing, swimming, or raising a child— you can read books, watch videos, listen to your family and friends, and gather a lot of information about how to bike, ski, swim, and parent, but you will need to do it to learn it and know it.

A different kind of learning is needed in addition to book learning and that is **procedural learning**. Procedural learning is a combination of the explicit and implicit acquisition of skills. I can help you gain the explicit part of procedural learning in sharing my experience and knowledge about people I have coached and what to expect along the way to entrepreneurship. Additionally, it is useful for you to listen to supportive success stories of other private practice business owners, as they can offer useful insights too (we'll cover informational interviewing in Chapter 7). Explicit is accessible by recall. You are able to remember through past experience how to do something. The implicit aspect of procedural learning in the acquisition of skills is buried in the memory as the experience on how to do something. You can't explain how you know. You just know.

SUMMARY

Committed action done in alignment with your values will most likely require different choices during the life cycle of your private practice business. Making a choice based on your values is a major protective factor in being able to stay the course through the noise in the environment and the noise in your mind. Committed action permits you to effectively navigate the challenges of the first two stages of your business, forming and storming, when the temptation to stall out with the trap of shoulding is strong. The first two stages of forming and storming lead to the beginning stages of actually birthing your private practice sweet spot, and they set the stage for increasing the odds of success at later developmental stages. If you are still not sure or are feeling like you are sitting on the fence, the next chapter includes a tool used in the financial sector and in the mental health addiction recovery field to get you prepared.

CHAPTER

5

Preparedness

Perhaps you have heard of a process called cost-benefit analysis (CBA). It is used worldwide in the public and private sectors to balance the monetary costs and benefits of programs and policies. CBA is a decision-making tool with techniques originating in Europe in the 1840s. Within the field of psychology, CBA is used with Motivational Interviewing as a way to talk about the stages of change in addiction recovery. Also, Rational Emotive Behavior Therapy (REBT) utilizes the process of cost and benefit analysis to enhance motivation. Within REBT benefits are behavioral reinforcers and costs are viewed as punishers. Now, I encourage you to complete a cost-benefit analysis even if you are 99.9 percent sure you are going to open a private practice business.

I am providing a starter Cost-Benefit Analysis Chart below. As you complete it, stay attuned to your level of excitement. Notice if you get fired up or cooled down. The best way to begin this chart is with a brief mindfulness exercise to heighten your awareness levels. Close your eyes and focus on your breath. Find a place in your breath that is easy to focus on, such as the rise and fall of your chest or the tip of your nose where your breath begins its journey into your body and exits. Sometimes I like to listen to my breath. Find an easy place to turn your focus toward your breath for sixty to ninety seconds before completing the chart.

COST-BENEFIT ANALYSIS CHART

You may download the Cost-Benefit Analysis Chart from my website, or use a separate piece of paper. Within the field of psychology it is customary to start with benefits when exploring behavior change.

Options	Benefits	Costs
Launch a private practice business	**Short Term:** What are some immediate benefits you will enjoy? Think in both monetary and non-monetary terms that include human well-being. **Long Term:** What are the possible long-term consequences of private practice that will be of benefit in your career/life? Think in terms of one year, five years, ten years.	**Short Term:** What are some immediate costs or losses you will experience? Think in both monetary and non-monetary terms that include human well-being. **Long Term:** What are some of the possible losses or costs to your career/life you are willing to accept in the time frame of one year, five years, ten years?
Pursuing an alternate career path outside of private practice	**Short Term:** What are some of the benefits you will experience right now by choosing not to go into private practice? This can be answered in monetary and non- monetary terms. **Long Term:** What are the long-term benefits you might experience in your life by not entering private practice?	**Short Term:** What costs will you incur right now by choosing to look elsewhere for a career path that does not include launching a private practice? These can be both monetary and non-monetary. **Long Term:** What will the costs possibly be over a one-, five-, or ten-year period in pursuing an alternate career path that does not include private practice?

You can change the questions around and ask what the costs and benefits might be for agency work. Another option might be to work in someone else's practice. There are multiple options for a career path and multiple ways to use the Cost-Benefit Chart.

The hard part is making a decision. Hence, analysis paralysis in the form of ambivalence or procrastination can quickly show up, and they have their own set of costs and benefits. I hope the chart teases apart some of the costs and benefits you might be contemplating. Frequently, one of the byproducts of completing a CBA chart is the appearance of motivation. See if you can connect to what motivates you. Is there a motivation to move in one direction or another?

Willingness is another aspect a cost-benefit analysis measures. One way of understanding willingness is to ask yourself what you are willing to pay to receive the benefits of entering private practice. The other way of looking at willingness is to ask yourself what you are willing to pay for the loss your decision will incur by not entering private practice. There is a price to pay for all decisions. Earlier I mentioned a technical term used in ACT called **experiential avoidance**. This is directly connected to willingness. Let's dig a little deeper into the connection.

EXPERIENTIAL AVOIDANCE

Experiential avoidance, in ACT terms, includes behaviors that take people off-course. The roots of experiential avoidance are developed from our survival skills—experiential avoidance is a hardwired behavior we practice when coming in contact with discomfort. Following is a story you might be familiar with, but it is worth repeating.

Cavemen on the Savannah

Once upon a time there were two cavemen who lived on the savannah in a cave overlooking beautiful, lush grassland. At the edge of the grassland lay a thick forest. The cavemen liked to gather blueberries, raspberries, and other fruits and vegetables from the plants of the grassland and from the edge of forest to sustain them. They had a routine. Every morning they would rise, and each caveman would begin to plan the day of food gathering. Each caveman looked out across the horizon from the ledge of the cave, hoping to spot something he could gather and eat for lunch.

Each caveman had a slightly different personality and predisposition. The first caveman's personality was rather carefree and happy-go-lucky. One day in his morning routine he spotted something in the distance that looked like a bush full of berries. He was excited to get going. He wanted to quickly hop off the cave's ledge and run across the savannah to gather delicious berries for lunch. Now, the second caveman was a worrier, an anxious sort of fella. That morning the first caveman said to his caveman buddy, "Hey, I think I see a blueberry bush. Let's go get those berries. It's a bit far, but I am hungry, and lunch will be here soon."

The second caveman expressed anxiety about the long trip across the savannah to pick berries from a bush he could not see very well. He said to the first caveman, "I think that thing you see in the distance looks more like a bear than a blueberry bush. Let's wait and see." Meanwhile, the carefree caveman hopped off the ledge and ran across the savannah toward the distant edge of the forest and the blueberry bush. A few hours lapsed and he returned with a stomach full of blueberries, with only a few berries for his buddy. Needless to say, the carefree caveman had a great lunch.

The next day the same thing happened. The first caveman spotted another bush in the distance, at a different location on the edge of the forest. He insisted his buddy come with him to gather blueberries for lunch. The first caveman ran off to get lunch while the anxious and skeptical caveman stayed behind listening to his hungry stomach growl. This time when the carefree caveman returned, he had nothing for his buddy because he had eaten all the blueberries before returning home.

On the third day, the first caveman spotted another bush in the far, far distance along the farthest edge of the forest. He was feeling lucky and was sure it was going to be another blueberry bush, although he could not see it very well. He nagged his buddy, "Come on! Let's go have lunch." The second caveman told the first caveman he thought the bush looked more like a bear. Off went the first caveman alone to have lunch. The second caveman waited and waited for hours and hours for his buddy to return. He did not.

What happened? This time instead of having lunch, carefree caveman became lunch.

How can this story be of benefit to you? The takeaway lesson: The reason you are here today is because you are a distant relative of the second caveman—the worrier. The anxious and skeptical caveman lived to reproduce and here we are today. Consequently, you and I are hardwired to be worriers. We are hardwired to be fearful and cautious, if not downright anxious. We have a strong tendency to play it safe so we don't become lunch.

How does the story tie into your business? See if this rings true for you: Launching a private practice business or expanding your private practice can bring out the fearful, anxious, worried skeptic. Speaking in general terms, we all have a zone of comfort—routine and safe. We go about our daily lives on automatic. This is normal. There is no way you or I or anyone else can focus on every little detail or decision each moment throughout the day. It would be exhausting. However, change the routine and boom! We become more alert. We perk up. Change the routine too much and we experience fear at some level. This may show up as anxiety, apprehension, ambivalence, depression, anger, and so on and so forth.

Our mind is superior at keeping us safe and looking for environmental threats. The problem-solving mind will generate thoughts to keep you in your comfort zone. These thoughts play out in the form of experiential avoidance.

We avoid going across the savannah to the blueberry bush. We avoid risk. We live with hunger rather than take a chance. The problem is we respond as if a bear is going to eat us alive and our safety is at stake. In today's modern world, experiential avoidance is an unwillingness to have uncomfortable feelings, to not becoming lunch for a bear. The way out of this dilemma is to move to a neutral observer position. The way back toward empowerment is to notice. To become aware. To practice mindfulness. Can you observe your inner reactions and describe them in a nonjudgmental way? Can you let them be there and bring self-compassion into the mix?

Below is a script that can help you move to the observer spot. I like to use it with counseling and coaching clients. Fill in the blank with your specific anxiety, worry, or fear. I'll share one of the fears I face: I am going to fail.

"I Am Having the Thought" Defusion Script[13]

Step 1) I am having the thought that: I am going to fail.

Your turn: I am having the **thought** that:_____[with your eyes closed, say it three times to yourself].

Step 2) I am **noticing** I am having the **thought** that:_____ [with your eyes closed, say this three times to yourself].

Step 3) I am **NOTICING** that I am **noticing** that I am having the **thought** that:_____[with your eyes closed, say this three times to yourself].

How was that? The above script is useful to create cognitive distance between your thoughts and your observer self. The script is *not* meant to get rid of the thought or the feelings associated with the thought. The defusion exercise allows you a few moments, which is like distance in the form of time, to connect to your values and make choices leading you toward your value-based goals. An extra benefit of being in an open position of willingness is that therapist burnout decreases and creativity increases.[14]

I want you to meet Evelyn and hear her story. She joined my coaching group and worked hard at designing a website and defining a niche.

She ordered business cards and set up an office to share with a supportive friend. Evelyn is an athletic coach at a high school. She is also trained as a therapist. During her coaching sessions with me her eyes filled with tears as she expressed a passion to bring athletic coaching and therapy together and incorporate them into an effective therapy to help teenage girls. She had a unique talent and a unique practice helping girls find emotional strength through connecting to their physical strength.

Evelyn worked hard for months on laying a solid foundation. She was close to launching her practice, when, to my surprise, she came in one day without warning and immediately quit the coaching group. I felt terrible for her. She had worked so hard. I probed with questions and encouraged her to reconsider. In the process I learned she was facing a huge roadblock in the form of a recurring thought, one with a long history in her life. A thought that left her feeling vulnerable. The thought contained fear and shame: *What will people think of me. I am not good enough.* My heart hurt for her. I knew she was hungry to fulfill her dreams.

At times like this, persistence and perseverance are crucial. I understood she was not ready. At the same time, I knew she possessed a wonderful gift. She had a way of teaching young girls by helping them feel strong and capable. Evelyn's insecurity, uncertainty, lack of confidence, and "not good enough" thoughts and feelings were her roadblocks to fulfillment. Fear controlled her. She acted like the worried caveman on the savannah as if a bear were going to eat her alive. When fear shows up in your life, as it does in all people's lives including mine, reconnect to your dreams and ask yourself, *What will happen it I persist?*

SHOULDING AND WHAT IFS

We all grow up with rules about good and bad behavior. It is how we become civilized and learn how to function in groups such as our families, at school, and at work. We grow up with rules about gender and aging as well as religion, community, and politics. These rules are given to us in the form of verbal instructions; this is the gift of language. We also learn about the rules of behavior through observational learning. We adopt values grounded in our family culture, religious culture, school culture, community culture, national culture, and beyond. We internalize these rules. The dark side of language around rules is that some rules show up as "should" thinking. I touched on shoulding in Chapter 4.

The problem with rule-governed behavior (shoulding behavior) is it cuts us off from awareness and the freedom to choose what we truly desire. We become so focused on rule-following, we become immune to clues in our environment about other options. Sometimes these are internal clues that show up in our bodies as an increase of energy. If you notice a lack of motivation, check your beliefs about the rules you buy into. When we are stuck in following the rules, we feel less inspired. I see this with clients who exhibit dread. Dreaded rules evoke fretfulness in the form of worry, anxiety, and apprehension. External clues also remain obscure. We miss the indicators in the environment that present us with options in the way of opportunities. If this happens, I recommend you do something different. Anything different will take you out of the shoulding zone.

I want to be clear here about rules. I am not advocating anarchy. I am advocating for your dreams.

Entrepreneurial creativity happens when we color outside the lines. Adhering to the shoulding rules, you might catch yourself living a life designed by others rather than living a life of your own. Let me connect this to the values held within the therapeutic relationship. Isn't changing what we hope for our clients? They often come in for therapy, and we walk with them into the dark places of their life. We tell them it takes courage. It also takes courage to enter private practice.

A close traveling companion to shoulding rules are *what ifs*. What ifs hook you with the trepidation of entering the unknown. One of the major questions ACT asks of us as therapists and asks of our clients is to look at how thoughts, feelings, sensations, or urges serve us. How does the *What if...?* thought function? In general, does it help you engage in behaviors that will move you toward creating a thriving private practice? Or are you engaged in behaviors that move you away from the discomfort of what if...what if I fail? What if something goes wrong? If you find what ifs taking you off track, take a breath. Lift your eyes and see your surroundings. Smell the air. Feel the air. Notice your feet on the ground. Take another breath. We all dance with being on and off track. Just like shoulding. Do something different—anything.

I have first-hand experience with shoulds and what ifs. While writing this book, there were times I felt more urgently that I should be dusting, cleaning, cooking, or doing laundry—so all my chores were done, and only after that could I take time out of my day to write. You guessed it; there are always more chores. Cleaning was my shoulding story. The what-if showed up when I finally sat down at my computer to write content for the book. What if my peers read my book and they thought it was terrible? What if my book doesn't sell? Then I cycled back into shoulding. I should write better and should know more. I'll bet you have experience with shoulding and what ifs. That's OK. You can still do the work.

Knowing about defusion skills, the caveman on the savannah, shoulding, what ifs, and how to conduct a cost-benefit analysis prepares you for the inevitable paralysis that comes with fear, apprehension, and playing it safe anytime you take a risk.

SUMMARY

When your mind says to run like hell and save your ass or the bear will eat you alive, take a moment and notice. Notice your thoughts, feeling, urges, and sensations. Experiential avoidance is at play in an attempt to avoid the unavoidable experience of discomfort. Be prepared for factors that help you along or hinder you. Your problem-solving mind is working hard at keeping you alive. Provided in this chapter is a Cost-Benefit Chart you can choose to use in combating analysis paralysis. You have a script to help you with thoughts that try to boss you around. Shoulding and what ifs are traps that keep you stuck. After reading this chapter, I hope you are at a place of being open and willing to move forward. I say this to you: The terrain is sometimes bumpy on the way to launching a private practice, and being prepared will help you navigate the terrain. You want to have a strategy in place to keep going when the going gets tough. To that end, we'll talk about motivational strategies next.

CHAPTER

6

Motivational Strategies

Private practice is a marathon, not a sprint. How do you keep yourself going when you feel low on fuel? Motivational speaker and author Zig Ziglar[15] offers a philosophy of motivation: "People often say that motivation doesn't last. Well, neither does bathing. That's why we recommend it daily."

Think back through your history and recall the times when you felt like a project might be too much, yet you accomplished your goal. What sustained you along the way? You will do best if you have a foundation of supportive people to encourage you. The chances of burnout are diminished with a team of allies.

ALLIES

Gathering allies may seem like common sense. Allies help us stay motivated when we feel discouraged or disillusioned. They help us with being accountable; we can confide in them, and that alone helps us take responsibility for our success with follow through or the lack of follow through. However, we often overlook allies when going into a solo practice. Many people end up isolated from their community when they go into a solo practice.

We all want somebody on our side and in our corner. Choose wisely who you put there. Surround yourself with people who believe in you and want to support you in your calling. Surround yourself with people who will kindly give you an honest opinion. Remember gatekeepers might not be your best choice. Take time to make a list of people who have the qualities to fit into your tribe of allies, then carefully nurture those relationships.

Where to find allies? Allies can be found among your family, friends, colleagues, former instructors, students, or coworkers. You know they are with you, not against you. A true ally can help when you feel confused with what direction to take by listening without giving advice. Allies are true gifts. Turn to them to refresh your enthusiasm and motivation. Keep in mind reciprocity is part of the relationship.

MOTIVATION AND INSPIRATION

Most people think inspiration and motivation are the same and use the words interchangeably.[16] What is the difference? **Motivation** is derived from the word "motive," which is to have a reason to do something. Be clear about the *reasons* for going into the business of private practice—this will help you stay motivated. Motivation is like a carrot in front of you. **Inspiration** fuels something deep within you. "Inspire" is to "infuse with excitement." It comes from Latin meaning *to breathe or blow into*. To be inspired is a process of being mentally stimulated to do or feel something, especially to do something creative. Inspiration feels like a flame burning from the inside, and motivation feels like a force pulling you forward from the outside.

There is no one formula to stay or get motivated. We all have different tools, and you might find something motivates you today but does nothing for you tomorrow. It's a good idea to have an arsenal to inspire you.

You need both inspiration and motivation for the long haul. Some people are inspired by daily affirmations delivered to their inbox. Others have favorite songs, poems, movies, or public figures. I am inspired by the words of Maya Angelou, an American poet, memoirist, and civil rights activist: "My mission in life is not merely to survive, but to thrive; and to do so with some passion, some compassion, some humor, and some style."[17] Those words energize me to stay motivated about my mission in life.

A little side story: I am named after Brenda Starr, a character from the comic strip *Brenda Starr, Reporter*, created in the 1940s. She was portrayed as a glamorous, adventurous reporter who traveled the world. The strip no longer runs (newspapers are a dying industry), but she was my ally through-out my youth and early adulthood. She was my role model. I was inspired and motivated by her stories. I wanted to be just like her. Why am I telling you about Brenda Starr? You can be anyone you identify with who elevates you toward being your best self. Set the stage for your future by identifying who and what inspires and motivates you—the people can be real or imaginary.

If you are inclined to be of a humanistic ilk, you might find what I am saying sounds a lot like Abraham Maslow's hierarchy of needs from his book *A Theory of Human Motivation*. In the '60s, Maslow expanded his theory beyond self-actualization to helping others become self-actualized. Is private practice going to be the vehicle that propels you toward self-actualization and transcendence?

Motivation can also be found in partnering with other people to work toward common goals. If you plan on partnering with someone, consider making that part of your business plan (see BookSweetSpot.com). You don't need details; you only need to include partnerships as part of a growth strat-egy. Partnering doesn't necessarily have to be formal or stay the same person in a partnership. In the beginning of my private practice I found people to facilitate workshops with, go to networking events with, and share in marketing projects. Questions to ask yourself when looking for partnership:

- Do you want to facilitate groups or workshops? Who would complement your knowledge and skills?

- Who would you like to have coffee or tea with? Then invite them to attend a networking event with you.

- Do they already attend networking events? Ask if you can join them.

- Do you know somebody who writes a blog? Invite them to be a guest blogger on your website and vice versa.

If you think a partner will be an ally in the supportive, good-listening skills sense, think again. You both need to have your own team of allies. It is difficult to drag someone with you as both partner and ally. By the way, not all partnerships went smoothly for me as I stumbled along looking for the right combination of people. Be prepared to let go of what does not work. Most of all, get your motivational ducks in a row early on. It is sure to pay off in the long run.

REWARD YOURSELF

Following is what I planned out for the first year in private practice. My weekly reward was a half-day hike in the nearby foothills of the Rocky Mountains. I love being in nature and taking the time to hike felt like a luxury. It boiled down to rejuvenating myself and clearing my mind with mindful walking. For my monthly reward, I bought a pair of inexpensive earrings. For my one-year anniversary of being in private practice, I rewarded myself with a one-week vacation—not a big expensive one. I like new places, and there are plenty of cool towns in Colorado I yearned to visit.

Reward yourself with a treat if this is what keeps your candle burning bright. Rewards can be a monthly or weekly massage, pedicure, hike, or other pleasure. Rewards can be small for small projects and larger for larger projects. Remember when you were a kid and your homework was handed back to you with a star or sticker? I use a similar method on my to-do list. Simply write "done" next to the task.

Make a reward plan. Switch it up if it needs tweaking. What felt rewarding yesterday might not feel rewarding today or tomorrow. We become habituated.

Tooting your own horn with an ally can be rewarding. A little bragging with a confidant feels exciting. Really, it is OK to toot your horn regardless of what the lessons were from your childhood. When you reach a goal, share it with an ally (see Chapter 2 or your Nine Goals in 90 Days worksheet downloaded from BookSweetSpot.com for more on goals). You need to know how to measure your progress, even if you don't set goals exactly as I suggest. Research on motivation indicates setting clear goals with deadlines that include some feeling of risk increases motivation and satisfaction. Do you like the feeling of satisfaction? I do.

KEEP A JOURNAL

Keeping a journal dedicated to the topic of your journey into the world of private practice entrepreneurship is another way to stay motivated. Although the journal might be dedicated to your private practice journey, you can write about any topic. Warning—don't use client names in your journal (initials are OK). Keep your journal private and date your entries. Journaling is not only a wonderful therapeutic tool, but it also is a useful business tool as you grow into your business and your professional identity. Journaling allows for reflection and focus. Kay Adams, the founder of the TW (Therapeutic Writing) Institute, provides five easy tips for journaling, which she organized into the acronym WRITE:

- **W**hat do you want to write about? What's going on? How do you feel? What are you thinking about? What do you want? Name it.

- **Review** or **reflect** on it. Close your eyes. Take three deep breaths. Focus. You can start with "I feel…" or "I want…" or "I think…" or "Today…" or "Right now…" or "In this moment…"

- **I**nvestigate your thoughts and feelings. Start writing and keep writing. Follow the pen/keyboard. If you get stuck or run out of juice, close your eyes and re-center yourself. Re-read what you've already written and continue writing.

- **T**ime yourself. Write for 5-15 minutes. Write the start time and the projected end time at the top of the page. You may use the timer on your phone or a personal digital assistant (PDA) to keep track.

- **E**xit smart by re-reading what you've written and reflecting on it in a sentence or two: "As I read this, I notice…" or "I'm aware of…" or "I feel…" Note any action steps to take.

Eye Can Exercise

In Chapter 8, I will cover how to make a vision board; meanwhile, I have a fun, easy, and quick project for you to complete this week that is similar: an Eye Can. All you need is a 16-ounce, clean, empty vegetable or fruit can; one magazine; and some rubber cement glue. Sort through the magazine and cut out images of eyes and glue them onto your empty can. There you have it—an Eye Can. Use it as a pencil- or penholder at home or work. Make two and keep one at home and one at work. Stay motivated with a reminder to yourself that "I (or Eye) Can" do it.

People I coach have used the Eye Can for affirmations and as a gratitude receptacle. One lady filled her Eye Can with her favorite affirmations; every day she pulled one out to read to herself. Of course, to do this you need to spend some time writing a dozen or so affirmations on small pieces of paper to put in the can. Another gal used her Eye Can to keep gratitude scripts for her workday. How will you use your Eye Can?

LEAVE A TASK INCOMPLETE

Have you heard of the Zeigarnik Effect? A Russian psychologist, Bluma Zeigarnik, was fascinated with waiters who could remember long and complicated food orders. Once the waiters completed serving the food, they forgot the order. Researching this memory phenomenon, Zeigarnik determined that at the core of the effect is the discomfort experienced with incompleteness. Once something is complete, it is easily forgotten. The Zeigarnik Effect is like an itch screaming to be scratched, drawing our attention back to finish an incomplete project or task. This is one of the reasons multitasking does not work—our attention is drawn away from being fully present on any one task.

How can the Zeigarnik Effect help you stay motivated? Leave something for the next day to complete. It might be your to-do list with only one item to start the day. I use the Zeigarnik Effect while writing by not completing a paragraph. I experience the discomfort of incompleteness and feel motivated to get back to the task of writing. Well, I have to admit I am motivated to quiet my discomfort. It is soothing to come back and work on my project. Consequently, the Zeigarnik Effect helps with procrastination. Give it a try. Don't finish reading to the end of a paragraph. Stop in mid-paragraph and see what happens.

SUMMARY

Motivation is an ongoing, multifaceted practice every business owner depends on. Private practice and entrepreneurship are not a nine-to-five job with a boss who sets the expectations of performance standards. Having the energy to be productive in the art of therapy and the administrative tasks required to run a business takes motivation. Finding the right combination will be a trial-and-error process to see what works for you. This chapter covered some tried-and-true methods; you are sure to find others. One way to learn more about different motivational strategies and what inspires people is with an informational interview, covered in the next chapter.

CHAPTER

7

Informational Interviews

Talking with a variety of business owners will round out your ability to decide if private practice is for you. If you have never heard of or conducted an informational interview, you are in for a treat. You risk very little, with a chance to gain a boatload of useful information.

One of the purposes of conducting informational interviews is to learn how people maintain both the roles of the therapist and the private practice business owner—of helper and entrepreneur—and still have a balanced life while making a livable income. We all have ideas about private practice. Until you are walking in the shoes of being a private practice business owner and a therapist, you can only guess what it is like. Informational interviews fill in the gap of the unknown. An informational interview is a reality check garnered from real people.

Informational interviews are an excellent tool anytime you want to start a new project or expand your business. Talk to those who have gone before you. No sense in reinventing the wheel. If you want to do podcasts, start vlogging, or write a book, talk to someone who has done so. As you conduct the interview, look for areas of strengths and weaknesses in the person you are interviewing and within yourself. Keep an open mind about how others navigate their weaknesses as possible solutions to your own weaknesses. You might even meet your future mentor or future business coach while conducting informational interviews (more on mentors in Chapter 15).

You can frame the informational interview in the context of an intake interview where you want to discover what is happening in a person's life. Be objective and take good notes. Listen and ask questions in a nonjudgmental manner. You want to gather as much information as possible.

What are you most curious about? What are your greatest fears? What was their greatest challenge? Do they have a business plan, and did they start out with a business plan? What do they know now that they wished they knew in the beginning? These questions act as the catalysts to the kinds of questions you want to craft for the informational interview.

CANDIDATES AND ETIQUETTE

A byproduct of an informational interview is growing your connections and building a community. Be clear—this is not the *purpose*, only a byproduct. The biggest benefit is a reality check before you take the plunge.

Who would be the good candidates for you to interview? Conduct informational interviews with people you want to emulate or who would make effective mentors. They can be people who inspire and motivate you. We all need to have committed mentors and inspiring role models, even when we think we already know how to create success and have it made. The most successful therapists often are pressed for time and have busy schedules, however. It can be difficult to get an appointment with them.

I strongly recommend you select a total of six people. Consider interviewing a newbie in private practice, someone who has been in private practice less than two years, and a person who has been in practice for about five or six years. Include a therapist who has been in private practice for over 25 years as well. People will be at different developmental stages in their private practice. Reflect on the fact they entered the world of private practice in historical terms in their own lives and historical terms in the field. A person launching a private practice today might brand their practice and actively market it, while a person who entered private practice thirty years ago launched in the Golden Age. They might be generalists and not even have a website.

Other people to consider interviewing are therapists who are all self-pay and others who are on insurance panels. Consider people who have a specific niche, such as gifted teens or couples struggling with infidelity. This process allows you to gather well-rounded information.

Before the interview, do your homework. Check out their website. Read their bio. Check out their LinkedIn account. Do a Google search. Make knowing your interviewee and setting the agenda priorities. Remember they are doing you the favor. If you get nervous and feel like backing out, practice the defusion script in Chapter 5. Also, you can start with someone you know who will be more comfortable for you to interview, then build up to the interviews that feel more intimidating.

Be respectful of your interviewee's time. Ask how much time they have available in advance and stick to the time allotted. It is safe to assume a twenty- to thirty-minute phone interview or face-to-face meeting is reasonable. I like face-to-face so I can see their office as an expression of who they are as a therapist (plus decorating ideas).

If you are meeting in person, take a token gift such as a small package of candy. I like jelly beans. Immediately after the meeting, complete a thank you card. Have the cards with you so you can write a thank you as soon as the meeting is over. Also, let them know you will be sending them an invitation to your grand opening, if and when you decide to enter private practice.

Whatever you do, *don't* ask for client referrals. You are not there to get business. You are there to get information and build a professional relationship.

Do ask for their business card and/or a brochure. Ask if they have a newsletter or blog you can subscribe to. You can learn a lot about the dos and don'ts of blogging by following other people. Making comments on their blog is a way to stay connected and build community.

Do you connect with them on other social media platforms? It is OK, as long as you don't act like a stalker. If you are not sure, ask first. If the person has a LinkedIn account, you can connect with them and follow their posts, as LinkedIn is a business-to-business platform.

With informational interviews, you are actively doing community building. One caveat for the stance of an informational interview: be transparent.

INFORMATIONAL INTERVIEW QUESTIONS

Below are some ideas for interview questions to consider. Tweak them for your interests and for each person you plan to interview.

1. What attracted you to this career and to enter private practice? Did you have a prior career? If so, why did you switch careers?

2. What has changed about your passion and zest as a therapist and business owner?

3. What do you like most about what you do, and what would you change if you could?

4. Are there paid externships I could participate in that would

prepare me for the business aspects of private practice? Who helped you? May I contact them?

5. How do you see the profession changing in the next five to ten years? Specifically, in the area of private practice? How are you preparing for the change?

6. Where is the greatest growth potential for a specialty in this profession?

7. What are some of the biggest challenges facing our profession today?

8. What professional organization(s) would you recommend I join?

9. What do you read—in print and online—to keep up with developments in your field?

10. If you were just getting involved now, what would you do to put yourself on a successful trajectory?

11. What's a typical day like for you?

12. What's unique or differentiating about you? How do you stand out in the crowd?

13. How has your career differed from your expectations? What have been the greatest moments and biggest challenges?

14. What works best in attracting clients?

15. If you had only one piece of advice to give me, what would it be?

16. Is there anything I haven't asked that you think is important to know?

17. Who would you suggest I interview after you?

To generate more questions, look over the business plan you've started. Write any questions that come to mind in your journal or on a separate sheet of paper.

Once you have tweaked your questions, call the person or persons to set up an interview. Be prepared with a message for your request. Tell them your name. Tell them how you came to call them, such as a friend referral, online directory, or Google search. It's a good idea to develop an introductory script, as they will wonder who you are and what you want.

Ask if they can talk a few minutes. When I cold-call someone, I always ask if they have a minute to spare right now. Then you can say something like, "I would be honored if you are willing to grant me an opportunity to conduct an informational interview about you, your career path, and your private practice. It will only take twenty to thirty minutes maximum of your precious time, unless you are available for a longer interview. The reason I would like to interview you is to gather information about being both a therapist and an entrepreneur. We can do the interview over the phone or in person."

FOLLOW UP: HANSEL AND GRETEL
CONTACT FORM AND JOURNAL

After the meeting, make sure to follow up. If you said you'd send an article, contact someone, or do something, make sure to do what you said you would. A lesson I learned early on is to under promise and over deliver. If you want to continue the relationship, figure out how to stay in touch. Again, if they have a blog, that is one way to stay connected. If there is no chemistry, move on. Either way, mail them a thank you card.

Do not send an email. I have firsthand experience with the importance of personally written cards versus emails. In my career at a Fortune 500 company as an employment recruiter, I hired hundreds of people and interviewed thousands of potential employees. That is a lot of people. The total number of cards people sent with notes of gratitude? Fewer than a dozen. Who do you think I remember? Even if there is no chemistry, sending a card makes you memorable. Your thoughtful card of appreciation makes you stand out in the crowd.

As you make connections, develop a system to track who, when, and where you met the person. It's important to nurture professional relationships just like a friendship. However, it's easy to get lost with information overload. The story of Hansel and Gretel inspired me to develop a way back to each individual relationship. *Hansel and Gretel* is a well-known German fairy tale written by the Brothers Grimm in 1812 about a young brother and sister. They are taken to the woods and abandoned in hopes they would be unable to find their way back home. The clever Hansel left clues with skipping rocks and eventually bread crumbs to help him find his way back. His system worked. I find my way back to nurture my professional relationship and grow my network through a Hansel and Gretel Journal. You can too.

At the time of printing, pricey software programs are available to track relationships. For the budget conscious new to private practice, start with my affordable system: a three ring binder and notebook paper. You may download a template from BookSweetSpot.com. Don't like the name? Call it something like Bread Crumbs or Skipping Rocks. Put the form into the three ring binder. Alphabetize the form by name. Your system needs to include the below information.

Name: if the person gives you a business card it will contain most of the following information. Simply staple it to the Hansel and Gretel form and make notes.

Date of first meeting and the event or introduction method. Luncheon, workshop, conference, neighbor, etc. Details are important but you don't need to go overboard.

Notes of topics discussed, both professional and personal. Examples include how long and what position with the company or private practice, or if the person mentions they like football or Ted Talks. Make a note on what stands out. Birthdays, anniversaries, children, movies, books; boss, coworkers, research.

Date to follow up with specifics and with method: phone, email, text and if you plan to meet again. It is crucial in building trust you absolutely follow through.

In the entrepreneurial world it is common knowledge that your network determines your net worth. The individuals in your network are social capital and as valuable as money. It is your therapeutic ability to build authentic trustworthy relationships that allows you to build your personal and professional network.

Have fun conducting informational interviews. You are actively taking steps to become part of a community and grow your network. Feel the excitement. Once you have completed an informational interview, take twenty to thirty minutes and journal about what you learned and what you still want to know. How crucial is the *still need to know*? Are you willing to move forward even if you don't have all the answers? Knowing you don't know is OK.

Facebook does not count as staying connected with your contacts unless it is a private and personal message. I am apprehensive to even go that route. I have the best luck with email. When sending follow-up email, keep messages short and concise. Make every effort to give a clue in the subject line about the topic of the email—in other words, a subject line that encourages the reader to open the email.

SUMMARY

Think of informational interviews and note-taking like an intake interview. You have the skills to do this based on your formal training. Think of the process as a shortcut around getting an MBA, from people who are in the trenches. The people you interview have a wealth of information. Your to-do list:

- Buy thank you cards for the interviewees.

- Make a list of six or seven candidates. Not all will be available. If they are not, ask for a referral to another candidate who might be available for an informational interview.

- Buy a three-ring binder.

- Format a Hansel and Gretel Contact Form for the binder, or download from my website. Print and insert it into the binder.

- Print interview questions and customize based on your need-to-know curiosity.

- Write a script for introducing who you are and your specific request.

- Make phone calls to schedule interviews.

- Buy some gourmet jelly beans or some other goody for giving as a gift if you meet a person in their office.

- Send thank you cards—paper ones—through the U.S. Postal Service.

- Follow up with any commitments you made.

You have made it through the first two sections, Anatomy of Change and The Starting Line. You are expanding your courage. In the next section, you will have a chance to build on what you have learned. You will discover what differentiates you from other therapists as you begin to define your identity and position in the community.

Positioning Your Passion

In Gabriel Gonsalves's blog post "The 4 Pillars of a Conscious Heart-Centered? Business," he describes "a business that exists solely for the purpose of supporting what is most important and meaningful to you, including a lifestyle that makes you feel fully alive and amazing, so that you can express your unique qualities, creative gifts and talents in service of others."[18] The big takeaway is you do not have to sacrifice yourself in the service of others. Many people who enter the helping and healing arts field are gifted with a deep sense of empathy and compassion, and often feel tempted to undercharge for caring services, among other self-destructive business practices. The temptation to give yourself away is a disservice to yourself, your loved ones, and your clients.

This third section includes interactive exercises to take a close look at your passions, then use those passions as a way to position yourself as a therapist and a business owner. It is challenging to clearly articulate what you do and what gifts you bring into the world. The exercises will provide a pathway to a clear version of your vision and mission as a heart-centered business. The significance of a clearly stated vision and mission is that together they act as a foundation in guiding almost all of your marketing and financial decisions.

Being authentic is part of the equation. In the next few chapters I ask you to complete exercises that answer the following questions: What energizes you? How do you live a balanced life that feels fulfilling and meaningful? In what ways are you unique? You will gain the knowledge of how you can remain true to your authentic self and build a successful business. No one else can decide for you, and no one else is responsible for how you direct your life. Maybe it sounds a little radical to believe you can be in control of your destiny. Perhaps this scares you. Perhaps it thrills you. Perhaps it's possible.

This radical idea of living a fulfilling and meaningful life is the bedrock of ACT. As you read the next few chapters, think of how you use a compass and a roadmap. You are setting the course to move in a purposeful, intentional direction.

Before we go on, let's get clear about a few business terms. The first term is **positioning**. This is a spot you occupy in the marketplace. The **marketplace** is either physical or virtual and generally is regulated by an agency or a standard of accepted practices to ensure quality and fairness of prices. It is the economic platform where prices of goods and services are determined by supply and demand.

Marketing experts have extensively studied branding and marketplace positioning. In the simplest terms, a brand is how people relate you to your uniqueness. Consequently, marketing a private practice is best when you are authentic. It is also the ethical way to market yourself.

Our goal in this section is to make marketplace positioning and branding intentional, while remaining true to you. As you progress through this section, you will discover what exercises yield important information you can harvest to position your passion, further clarify your niche, and create a recognizable identity (brand). Let's have some fun now with interactive experiential exercises. Many of these are great with clients too.

CHAPTER

8

What Matters Is What Differentiates You

In economic terms, differentiation refers to the competitive edge you have in the marketplace. It is the position you occupy in the mind of your potential client, your unique qualities that distinguish the differences between you and your fellow therapists.

The theory of differentiation was introduced to psychology by family therapist Murray Bowen, a pioneer in family systemic therapy. **Differentiation** is when an individual can maintain a strong sense of self while staying connected within a meaningful relationship. It is the ability to hold onto your identity, staying true to what you want out of life even when facing pressure to conform. Families with low differentiation will have members either enmeshed or distanced. Differentiation can be understood as your ego strength in knowing you have the capacity to fulfill your wishes and desires. And these concepts fit nicely into the framework of ACT with its focus on values and committed action.

Bottom line: your knowing who you are and being able to clearly state who you are and what you do will help you attract the kinds of clients you like to work with and at the same time will help reduce burnout. As I have mentioned before, building a successful private practice business is a marathon, not a sprint. Being able to sustain momentum for a marathon begins with being able to structure a private practice business that allows for you to have a balanced life.

Clarifying your values first will help you do this.

VALUES CLARIFICATION ACROSS LIFE DOMAINS

Life domains refer to specific, connected, and integrated aspects of living that are important to creating a fulfilling, meaningful, and vital life. Examples of life domains include family, work, community, leisure, spirituality, citizenship, parenting, friendship, and health. Each of us is in position to take full ownership of how we want to define a life domain and the importance of that domain in our life.

As we move through life, our perspective on the importance of the different life domains will change, as will the roles and rules within the life domains. The roles might include parent, partner, or entrepreneur. The rules about each of the roles in your life will be defined based on your understanding of what's important. Most often your life history will have an influence on what roles you deem important and what rules you want to bring to life within the roles. Within ACT, the roles and rules are flexible, so you maintain flexibility in the repertoire of behaviors to pick and choose from. Recall that in Chapter 2, we discussed **reality** and **relevance**. Knowing where you are today and what is relevant to your life paves the way to effective business planning. Essentially, it also paves the way to effective life planning; it helps you build a menu of life choices.

As you complete the exercises in this chapter, keep in mind the information you garner is food for conversations about your identity you will have with referral sources and potential clients. I want to be perfectly clear that what you are doing with these exercises is forming a professional identity that is in alignment with your core values, so you can communicate that effectively and clearly. Your answers are a guiding light for your business marketing practices. Overall, there are six exercises as a menu for you to choose from. Complete at least two.

The exercise below is a common exercise I use with therapy and coaching clients alike, and it is based on ACT values clarification. You can write in the book or download from my website.

Values Clarification Exercise

Begin by rating each life domain from a zero to ten, with zero indicating no importance to you and ten being of significant importance. You might discover there are domains of zero importance. That's OK. Then again, you might discover two rate a ten for importance. That is also OK.

Once you have rated the ten domains, choose your three or four top-rated domains and write a few words or a sentence or two about what is important to you about that domain. Another way to complete the second part of the exercise is to state the leading principles contained within the domain (what you think and feel are the central part of what guides your behavior in the domain). Eventually, you can use all this information as a springboard to help you identify people you want to work with. You can download the Values Clarification Exercise at BookSweetSpot.com.

___Health/Physical Well-Being

___Family Relations

___Intimate Relations/Marriage/Couple

___Community/Citizenship/Environment

___Parenting

___Spirituality

___Friendship and Social Relations

___Employment/Career/Work/Financial

___Recreation/Leisure/Fun

___Education/Training/Personal Growth

Example:

- 10 Health/Physical Well-Being:

  Maintaining my mental and physical health allows me to fulfill my needs and responsibilities in other important domains, leading to a high quality of life. I will do this with a balanced diet, regular exercise three times a week, and adequate sleep of at least 6 hours per night. I will see my doctor for a physical once a year to address any health problems and seek therapy as needed when struggling.

- 8 Family Relations_____

- 7 Intimate Relations/Marriage/Couple_____

- 6 Community/Citizenship Environment_____

- 2 Parenting_____

- 1 Spirituality_____

- 1 Friendship and Social Relations_____

- 9 Employment/Career/Work/Financial:

  Private practice is my current focus for employment and financial well-being. It allows me to fulfill a desire to be of service to people in the community and to bring financial benefits to my family. I am committed to being an honest and caring therapist and business owner with integrity. I believe in service and will donate time of one hour <<per week?pro bono as well as give money to a nonprofit as earnings allow.

- 10 Recreation/Leisure/Fun:

  Play and fun allow me to recharge and connect to my loved ones in ways that are healthy and reciprocal. I will spend time in nature camping and hiking while being a good steward of the environment. Relaxing activities such as movies and cooking will be a part of a weekly routine with my partner.

- 5 Education/Training/Personal Growth

As you complete the above values clarification, do you notice a pattern? Are there themes? If nothing jumps out, that is OK, as there are other exercises to further clarify your values and how to bring them to fruition so they can function as a compass and roadmap to fulfillment, meaningfulness, and purposeful choices in your behaviors. One more time: Connecting your values to your professional identity permits you to promote your private practice business in a manner that is genuine and authentic. It also elucidates who your ideal client might be as a good fit. The best part of values clarification is that you can set goals and take action in alignment with your values.

CONNECTING VALUES WITH GOALS AND OBJECTIVES

There is a strong connection between values, goals, and objectives. The difference between each is subtle. **Goals** are generally broad activities to be accomplished. **Objectives** are more specific activities that move you toward your goals. **Values** are a way of directing your goals and objectives. The metaphor of travel is a nifty way to look at the connections between the three.

How do you plan to travel? The vehicle you choose is the attitude you adopt. You can travel willingly or begrudgingly. You can travel with curiosity, even if you experience fear. You can travel with enthusiasm even if you experience insecurity. Attitude is a choice you make about the stance you will take on your journey.

Imagine you planned a trip from New York to San Francisco. There is no way you can predict what you will experience on your trip. You do know there are landmarks that indicate you're on or off track. These may come as a surprise, disappointment, fear, or confusion, but most of all they are indicators you're moving. Being open and willing to notice what you experience lets you adjust your course. Your values can guide you through whatever you experience.

Let's go on a journey. The idea of traveling or taking a journey with your values is a deep concept to grasp at first. I struggled with how I could put values into action in my life domains. For the purpose of illustration I am going to use the value of *kindness* as a way of traveling on a journey toward a particular direction, like going west. Here's the big question to ponder: Do you ever arrive at a final destination of west? No. The value of kindness is the way, not the destination. You can get to San Francisco and still keep going west. That being said, there are goals along the way, such as traveling to or through Denver. Denver represents a goal, such as being kind to the neighbor with the barking dog today. The reality is you can go west/be kind indefinitely. And along the way you set goals and objectives. How many ways can you be kind in your different life domains that matter to you?

Since our values are influenced by our history, let's take some time to connect your past, present, and future. Complete the following interactive exercise adapted from the New England Regional Leadership Program (Center for Rural Studies) for an experiential understanding of important life domains and values. The exercise is designed to connect your life history by exploring your past, present, and future. Use your answers for your business plan. You will discover distinctive stories and wishes with aspects only you have that will illuminate a living experience that differentiates you from all others. It's your silver lining to your vision and mission statements clarifying your business identity. A few pages of notebook paper will be all you need to complete the exercise.

Past, Present, and Future Exercise: Part One[19]

1. Take a few minutes to describe something that you do really well (this can be anything: hobby, work, craft, sport). Write about why you think you do it so well and about what "feels right" about it. Speculate about what makes this particular thing such a success with you.

2. Take a few minutes to write about a moment that inspired or impressed you, that caused you to pause, think, and make some kind of change or resolution. Describe what you were feeling and thinking at the moment when this happened and allow the drama of the moment to take its time. Also describe the change that happened in you after that moment.

3. Imagine that you have been asked to pass along a special secret to future generations, the secret of life you have learned over many years. Each person's secret is unique, and the secrets are being

recorded so no potential wisdom is lost. You are passing your secret along to unknown future people, so as you write, you want to use the clearest and most descriptive language possible. Write about this secret of life, stating it both directly and with the use of metaphors or examples.

4. You admit that you do not know everything, that there are still questions you cannot answer. However, imagine that you are presented with the opportunity to have any question answered. Write about the things you muse about and describe the questions you would present to a source of knowledge through this extraordinary opportunity.

5. Describe a success in your recent past that came as the culmination of hard work and dedication. This does not have to have been something that took a long time, just something that you kept working at until it was right. What were the elements of the work that made the outcome a success? Tell this story as a parable—an example illustrating a lesson.

Go back and highlight key words and phrases, looking for items of importance or recurring themes. Look for times when you took a particular ethical stance that held deep meaning.

Past, Present, and Future Exercise: Part Two

The questions in Part One are structured to help you develop sensitivity to the influences that shape you. As you read on, take time to ponder the purpose of the writing assignment with comments from Lois M. Frey, a contributor to the exercise, on each question.

- **Purpose of writing assignment (Question 1):** The areas of life that you do well or that seem naturally right to you are possible sources of your most basic values, but try to discriminate between physical talent and what "feels right" about it for clues about values.

- **Purpose of writing assignment (Question 2):** Moments of inspiration that cause a change are moments that affect you deeply and shape values related to the experience.

- **Purpose of writing assignment (Question 3) and (5):** Questions in which you are asked to pass along wisdom or lessons are directly related to what you value in life.

- **Purpose of writing assignment (Question 4):** Your questions about life indicate areas of growing or changing awareness about life, so are especially important to understand.

What have you harvested from the information in this exercise? Can you use it in planning a direction for your professional and your personal life? I continue to bring together professional and personal life, as they are connected, although they are different life domains. As we strive for balance, we can come back to our values. To piggyback on the writing assignment you just completed, I pose another question taken from my internship training. It's one of my favorites with new clients.

Magic Wand Intake Exercise

You probably heard a version of this exercise in your training days.

If you had a magic wand and nobody was looking, what you would do to make your world, your loved ones' worlds, your community's world, and society as a whole, a better place?

It's fun to ask other people this question as a conversation starter rather than a written exercise. You can break the exercise down into three, four, or five separate questions and explore your answers with another person. If you choose to do this exercise, notice what comes up in the conversation and the energy you feel. What lights your fire? This points you toward your ideal clients. The language and words that come up are excellent marketing verbiage.

TOOLS FOR CLARITY

At this point, you should have a good idea of your values and, hopefully, an idea of how to begin to bring them to life in connection to your private practice business. What next? What springs forth from values clarification that becomes part of your business identity, separating you from the crowd?

It is one thing to know your values and what matters to you, but can you deliver your services in a manner consistent with your values and in a manner that is comfortable and natural to you? Believe it or not, your uniqueness is your most marketable quality. On the next few pages, you will have a chance to explore how to breathe life into your values. How can you distill them into a memorable and meaningful brand without appearing artificial or trite? Remember you will be branded one way or another, so let's exert some influence over the branding process.

Your mind might be protesting that branding therapy is presenting it as a commodity. Many a therapist will emphatically state that therapy is not a commodity. Agree! Brand recognition and marketing is, however, the way our minds work to keep life simple. Just think of Nike. To have good recall we label, categorize, simplify, and stereotype every day. It is human nature. Count on it; you will become known as a particular therapist with a particular identity. Let me stress the importance of your taking this seriously if you want to thrive in your clinical work and thrive as a business owner. When you are clear about your professional identity, you can communicate it with conviction. In turn, you will attract the kind of people you work best with clinically. The extra benefit is you will stand out in the crowd and be memorable. I wish for you to thrive by finding that sweet spot where you can position yourself for success.

Following are a few more creative methods I use with great success. The small coaching groups I facilitated prior to writing this book found the following processes and activities beneficial. The process of branding takes an average of two to three months for a complete synthesis to occur. Don't let that discourage you. Creativity takes time but is so worth it. You can combine two or more methods—I combine them when I have a big decision to make or when I feel stuck. The purpose of the following methods is to get into the flow of creative solutions for your practice identity.

Percolating

In Chapter 1, you learned a little bit about **percolating**. Percolating is an easy yet somewhat mysterious method for finding clarity. It is a way of sitting inside confusion and chaos. Sitting with an open posture. Most of the time people want to escape and close off the discomfort of confusion and chaos. Percolating is the opposite of escape.

There are no specific instructions for percolating except to keep an open mind. It sounds counterintuitive, but trying to drill your ideas down limits creativity. Relax and let them expand. The process of divergent thinking can be understood from the same process in the study of epidemics and pandemics in small world networks.[20] Just like a disease spreads through networks, so do ideas spread through the neuro-networks of our minds as synaptic gaps link together in the propagation of information. Percolation is the how the World Wide Web came to be. Sir Tim Berners-Lee, the innovator of the World Wide Web, had an ambition to devise a system where creativity could flourish with machines in the same way as in the human mind.

Be patient with yourself. The time it takes to let your mind percolate to reach an "aha" moment depends on your ability to let your ideas
flow without inhibition. As I mentioned, you will need to set aside your
judging mind. No censorship allowed. Think of percolating as a therapy
process originated by Sigmund Freud's approach to free association.[21]
Let your mind wander about your values and life domains as you contemplate your ideas, as you argue with yourself about your ideas, and as you
flip them over to see them from different perspectives. Let your mind
percolate with the intention of letting your ideas be connected to your
values and the nature of your private practice. Track your percolation by
doing the following:

1. Record your random thoughts in one place. Use a small spiral
    notebook or a note-taking app on your smartphone. If you find
    yourself accumulating dozens of scraps of paper with notes scat-
    tered about, get a system that works for you.

2. Record your random thoughts immediately. This is important,
    as ideas are fleeting and can evaporate quickly, making it hard to
    recall them later. If you end up using scrap paper, be sure you put
    them all in one place at the end of the day.

3. KISS it. Write as little as possible and still make recall work.
    Details are not needed—KISS is: Keep It Simple Sweetie.

4. Review your notes as needed, but at least once a week.

Dreaming

Dreaming complements percolating. Night and day dreams hold meaning for us, just as our percolation thoughts do. We are fascinated with dreams,

so why not use them in the creative process? After all, we spend about a third of our life in sleep and about 20 percent of that in a dream state.

Pay close attention to the details. Notice the actors and the settings. Journal about your dreams.

Do you tend to forget what you've dreamed? Dream expert Lauri Quinn Loewenber[22]g says the most important thing to do to remember your dreams is to hold still for at least ninety seconds. Don't move. Don't even open your eyes. And, of course, keep a journal by your bed, to write them down after the ninety seconds. However, don't rush to interpret the dream too quickly. Allow yourself to soak the dreams in. Dreams can be literal, about day-to-day living, as well as be symbolic.

I gave myself plenty of time when I was going through the discovery phase for my private practice. I declare to you, take your time. It took me almost three months to arrive at my sweet spot. You are positioning your passion.

VISION BOARDS

If percolating and dreaming aren't doing the job, try a vision board. They are a lot of fun and yield a plethora of information, with a bonus of being a motivational tool.

Art therapists use vision boards, as do business owners, celebrities, and athletes. Vision boards are similar to visualizations, which fall into the realm of meditation, and meditation is a form of mindfulness. Hence, they are a tool to be used with the ACT core processes. You can make a new vision board every year as a creative and fun way to set your intentions for the year. They are great for new projects, products, or services too.

Vision boards are connected to your values, dreams, and goals. "Vision without action is merely a dream. Action without vision just passes the time. Vision with action can change the world," states Joel A. Barker.[23] Needless to say, you still need to have a game plan, then take action on your game plan.

Simply put, a vision board is a collage of things you want in life, experiences you desire, and people, situations, and feelings you want to manifest. Sometimes it's called a treasure map.

Vision Boards: What You'll Need

Poster board or an old picture you can glue over. You can go to a thrift store and pick out a cool frame with or without a picture. If you use poster board, the frame will keep the board flat and dust-free and will allow you to hang it on your wall.

Old magazines. If you've wanted to clean up your old magazine pile, here's a good excuse! If you don't have any, you can find magazines at a local thrift store. Also, check with friends to see if they have old magazines or ask your local library if they ever trash magazines. Choose magazines that have appealed to you in the past, as they're a treasure trove of images and words for your vision board. You can use scissors or tear the images out or a combination of both.

You can include almost anything: pieces of fabric, flower petals, leaves, shells, or rhinestones as well as rocks, nuts and bolts, small tools, and/or sprinkles of dirt. It takes a lot of elbow grease so if grease means something to you then add it to your vision board.

Glue. Don't use glue sticks, as the glue isn't stable (unless you're going to frame the vision board between a plastic cover and a cardboard backer, which should keep all the items secure). Personally, I like to use rubber cement glue.

Getting Started

Although your vision board is about the future, make it from the perspective of the present—as if you are living your ideal life professionally and/or personally right now. Create your vision board with symbolic images or the real deal.

I like to start with a slow, deep breath to get grounded in the present moment and clear my mind. If you want to use a little mental visualization image, try: *I have a successful private practice.* You may or may not have a goal or theme picked in advance; either way is OK. I find diving into the magazines and cutting or tearing images that appeal to me is the best way to collect ideas. I try not to include words. If you use words, be sure they resonate with your dreams. Hold your judgment about the images. If something appeals to you, add it to your pile. Cut out as many images as you want, even if you don't think you will use them. I want to repeat this: no need to critique what you find appealing; your brain, heart, and soul know what is important.

Sort the pictures into piles of themes:

- Feelings you are experiencing as if your future is now

- People who are in your life—family, colleagues, clients

- Travel and the places you are visiting

- Money and or images of prosperity

- Lifestyle you are living

- Professional goals you are working toward, such as enhancing your business with employees or products, becoming famous, or, like me, images of a book signing.

Once you feel you have enough pictures and they are sorted into piles, prioritize what must go on your vision board. Soften your focus and allow your thoughts, feelings, and intuition to guide you to the most important images and words. I am asking you to use your mindfulness skills to notice what comes up.

Next lay out your pictures without gluing. This helps you group the items in a pleasing manner and eliminate those that don't work for you. Also, you can write your own words and draw your own sketches for your vision board.

You are now ready to glue your pictures onto your poster board. If you are using a recycled framed picture from the thrift store, be sure you are gluing on the side you can put under the glass and the back of the picture is the blank side for the hanger. Once all your images are glued into place and dry, turn the vision board over to the reverse side and enter the date and a few affirmations. *Keep swimming* is an affirmation I wrote on the back of one vision board. *Follow my dreams* is another affirmation I included and one word: *beyond.* I ended up naming my private practice Creating Your Beyond. Cool!

Next find a trustworthy, supportive person to share your vision board with. Instructions for your chosen listener: first they listen then they ask you clarifying questions.

You are now ready to hang your amazing vision board where you'll see it. I made the mistake of putting my first vision board for this book on a wall that was obscured by a plant. Be purposeful. Repeat after me: Hang it where you can intentionally see it every day. Don't hide it behind a plant like I did. Once I moved my vision board to the right side of my home office door where I could eyeball it every day, I got motivated. Take a moment each day to focus on a portion of the board that calls to you.

Remember your Eye Can (Chapter 6)? You can place your Eye Can near your vision board. Why? So you can keep your eye on the prize. The prize, of course, is your success and fulfillment with a prosperous private practice. Staying motivated and focused on your dreams is a daily endeavor. With the vision board and Eye Can together, you can stay focused on what matters most in your life domains.

I challenge you to pause reading this chapter and get your supplies together to make your vision board. If you stop mid-chapter, you will have a chance to experience firsthand the Zeigarnik Effect (Chapter 6). You will learn how to parlay undone work into increased motivation and productivity. Give it a go. I'll be here when you are finished. Go on now—create your tomorrow today with a vision board.

Completing a vision board connects us emotionally to our dreams and goals. This gives us an opening to form effective habits and routines associated with successful leadership. You are in a leadership role as a private practice business owner. You are the CEO.

ONE OF A KIND

Welcome back! How did your vision board come out? I have seen a gazillion vision boards and there are no two alike. Your one-of-a-kind characteristics set you apart from all the other therapists in the marketplace, and they are your most marketable qualities. They let you claim a natural, fitting position in the community. If this feels like personal growth work, it is—and it is market-differentiating work. Go figure. It all ties together.

Claiming your position means being active in your strategies to convey your uniqueness. Remember we are taking your passions and creating a position in the marketplace for your private practice business. Positioning requires you to emphasize characteristics about yourself in comparison to other therapists and healthcare professionals. One of the reasons to do the comprehensive work of clarifying values is so you can clearly articulate your one-of-a-kindness. Let's take a quick rundown of positioning strategies. (Disclaimer: the following statements are only for illustration purposes.)

Positioning within a category: I offer concierge therapy and will come to you or meet you at your chosen location; for the busy professional or stay-at-home parent.

- Position according to product benefits: Get results with therapy using proven strategies with evidence-based methods (this is my positioning).

- Positioning according to product attribute: Effective trauma resolution with a set protocol by a trained and certified EMDR (Eye Movement Desensitization and Reprocessing) therapist.

- Positioning for usage occasion: Planning on marriage. Premarital counseling can get your relationship started on the right foot.

- Positioning along price lines: Affordable counseling with our interns. Sliding scales based on need.

- Positioning for a user: Have the _____ (fill in the blank) ability to counsel for teens/elders/children.

- Positioning along cultural lines: Being a female minority has its unique challenges. LBGTQ is my specialty. Man therapy.

- Positioning against other modalities: Mindfulness-based therapy is shown to work as well as medication for the treatment of chronic pain.

SUMMARY

You've completed a couple of exercises on values for the purpose of gaining a deeper knowledge of yourself and how this self-aware knowledge begins to fit into the marketplace. Values clarification is common within different therapeutic models. The point here is to highlight again that you have transferable skills. You also have some new lingo to go with your already-established knowledge base. By completing the values clarification exercises, you have expanded insights and thereby your business acumen. Eventually, you will have an identity that can be called your brand. I know, I know, you are not a commodity. We're just talking in business language. In the next chapter, we are going to use the metaphor of a superhero to further solidify your professional and business identity. You will need a coin and about four to ten colors of pens or pencils. Get ready!

CHAPTER

9

Superheroes—Get Your Cape On

Is answering the calling of entrepreneurship the role of modern-day super-heroes? What goes into the making of a superhero? You have the makings of a superhero if you are willing to answer the calling of entrepreneurship. Are you ready? What is your superhero power?

Many people describe entering the healing arts field as a calling. You have a backstory to how and why you are drawn to helping people. Most likely, your backstory is part of the gifts you bring into the relationship with clients. Based on research conducted by Alison Barr, a British counselor and coach, the backstory of many people called to the healing arts is the same story Joseph Campbell wrote about in his book *The Hero with a Thousand Faces* About 73.9 percent of people inspired to enter a field in the healing arts are survivors of emotional wounds and trauma, according to Barr.[24]

In this chapter, we want to make sure you are exactly the right person for your future clients.

There is a long history to the mythology of the hero's journey. In Greek mythology, the centaur Chiron, known as the "Wounded Healer," obtained an incurable wound from one of Hercules's poisoned arrows. The hurt from the wound transformed Chiron, giving him the power to heal. In recent history, the study of similar narratives centered on the transformational adventure about the wounded healer phenomenon began with Edward B. Tylor (1832-1917), the father of social and cultural anthropology. Tylor's interest was in understanding the function of religious narratives from a sociocultural perspective. His theories about cultural evolution influenced Campbell to direct his research of mythology toward the ubiquity of human suffering and the narrative of the transformational journey.[25]

It does not end here, as Campbell influenced the works of Otto Rank, a psychoanalyst who proposed the hero's journey or wounded healer was a psychological universal. Others caught up in the zeitgeist were Carl Jung with his archetypes and Rollo May with existentialism, plus many others in the field of psychology, philosophy, drama, and the arts. Where are we today with the hero's journey? Enter the superheroes.

Superheroes are the myths of modern-day culture. They offer individuals and larger societal groups different perspectives of understanding problems and how to solve them. Superheroes are prosocial and healers. However, they are not perfect. They come to their gifts through their vulnerabilities.

Superheroes let us test our moral compass. Who are your favorite superheroes? Who in *Star Wars*, *Harry Potter*, or *The Lord of the Rings* speaks to your inner superhero?

Let's meet a few of my favorite superheroes and the gifts they bring forth. Then I want to meet *your* superhero.

BEYOND GREEK MYTHOLOGY

Superheroes do their very best. They realize they are the only ones who are going to answer their calling. YOU are the only one who can answer your calling. Superheroes don't worry too much about belonging and fitting in. They know they are different. Trying to play it safe and fit in can take them way off track. Each superhero has their own unique style while being true to their authentic self. You could say the superhero narrative captures the essence of ACT in knowing what's important at the core of who you are. And I am going to say you have transcended your pain for the greater good. Being true to ACT is your willingness to take action to live a purpose-driven life, even when it is scary. The narratives of the wounded healer and the hero's journey show us the way.

Below is a list of superheroes and what they stand for. As you read the list, allow yourself to ponder your passions, your strength, your gifts.

- Spider-Man stands for responsibility, yet he lacks faith in himself.

- Green Lantern stands for duty, honor, peace, and justice.

- Captain America stands for protection of freedom and liberty. He is still human and can suffer harm and be killed.

- Hulk stands for self-control by harnessing the power of anger and hurt.

- Green Arrow and Wolverine represent that anyone can change and become a better human being.

- The Flash stands for progress, with science moving us forward to become better.

- Black Panther, T'Challa, was created in 1966 to address the lack of Black Americans as superheroes. Today he embodies genius with the ability to draw upon all previous knowledge, strength, and experience of former Black Panthers. His weakness is arrogance.

Let's start with Batman. He stands for justice. Fighting for justice is as timeless as the concepts of good and evil. Today we have a broad view of justice and injustice, because we are exposed to the concepts of justice through different platforms of media. The personality traits of superheroes change; Batman has become more eccentric to fit into pop culture, but his gift of being a force for justice remains the same.

A side of Batman we don't really focus on much is that he has his own set of weaknesses or vulnerabilities. Some say he needs a therapist.[26] He witnessed his parents getting brutally murdered when he was a child. He suffered. Loss. Grief. Insecurity. Guilt. These feelings plague him. Although he struggles with some of the painful aftereffects of trauma, within his painful wound the seeds of motivation grow. He has harvested justice from his suffering. What can you harvest from your pain or suffering?

Let's take a look at another superhero, Wonder Woman. Wonder Woman is depicted as taking a bold stance for truth about oppression. Truth and honesty do not have to be brutal. They can be feminine and strong. Her creator, William Moulton Marston, was a contributing inventor of the polygraph.[27] Marston created a superhero who carried his message, his passion, out into the world and inspired tolerance and truth. What passion are you willing to gift the world? Currently, Wonder Woman's character has transformed from liberated woman to represent feminism and lesbianism. Do you have a cause you are willing to champion?

There are *no* two superheroes whose style and gifts are exactly alike. You have your own style and gifts too. Your style will go through developmental stages, as do superheroes. It takes courage to open a private practice and become a business owner, to think like an entrepreneur while being true to your passion. Let me share another observation I have about superheroes. Listen carefully: they mess up!

Take Superman, for instance. When Superman rescues a plane from an impending crash, he is known to drop a few airplane parts hither and yon (as a butterfingers) while getting the plane full of people safely onto the ground. You do not have to have it all together to be a superhero or a private practice business owner. Take Jessica Campbell Jones of Marvel Comics. Her power is superhuman strength to protect people, yet her flaws include smoking and drinking. She is not perfect; she knows her flaws and takes full responsibility when she makes a mistake. The point is not that she smokes and drinks, but that she is flawed and knows it, and still uses her powers of protection. You do not have to be perfect to pursue your dreams. You need to be good enough. Perfection is the enemy of good enough. Your sweet spot is the intersection of your passion, your talent, and your motivation. If you have weaknesses and flaws, don't turn a blind eye to them, but know they are there and they are what makes you *you*.

In a short bit you will have a chance to design your own superhero. However, first let's practice a noticing skill to enhance your inner voice so you can tap into your wisdom. The Coin Flip Exercise is designed to help you develop the skill of careful listening to your inner knowing—beyond your thinking mind. You'll need a coin. Meet you back here in a few moments while you get one.

Coin Flip Exercise

Be curious about your visceral experience as you do this exercise. The key skill is mindfulness. Lean into your somatic experience. A word of caution: for the purpose of this exercise, flipping the coin is *not* a decision-making tool; it is an information-gathering exercise.

Take a minute to come into the full experience of the coin's weight in your hand and the texture of the ridges and indentations between your fingers;

notice the color of the material it is made of and the shape. Tap your finger on it and notice the sound. Now pick one side for "yes" to entrepreneurship and the other side for "no" to entrepreneurship. Notice how you feel when picking heads or tails. Notice what shows up in your body…and if your mind tries to distract you. Close your eyes for a moment, take one or two breaths, then open your eyes. Flip the coin into the air so it will land on the floor and take notice of how you feel…the somatic and visceral experience. Notice these in that fleeting moment as the coin bounces on the floor and comes to rest on heads or tails. Notice the flash of excitement or dread—notice the lightning bolt quickness of a message from within. If you felt nothing, that sometimes happens. You can try this on another day or with a different question.

The coin flip is not going to make the decision for you. You have the freedom to choose. And I want you to make the best choice for who you are and what you want. Remember the coin flip is simply a way to gather information about your inner feelings of vitality in connection to what works for you. The task here is to be mindfully aware of what comes up with the toss. Another thing I watch for is whether the body tilts forward or pulls backward. Try a couple of flips but don't overthink it.

Your Inner Superhero Exercise

Who is your favorite superhero? You are! Entrepreneurship as a superhero calling is daring and creative. You can live your passion. You can stand with your passion in the world. Tell me again: Why are you here? What is your life's purpose? What floats your boat? What fuels your energy? You have gifts and you have a responsibility to bring those gifts into the world. You are a superhero. Now take some time to journal in self-exploration. Jot down your answers to the following questions:

- You are a superhero! How does it feel?

- You have a special power—a gift. How does it feel being responsible for bringing those gifts to life?

- What attracts you to the above statements?

- What repels you about the above statements?

- Anything else?

Is there a "yes/no" or "push/pull" struggle? Remember the coin flip. Do you notice your visceral experience? Almost every person I have worked with experiences the yes/no struggle, including me. Sometimes I get off track trying to soothe the arguing voices of yes and no. Be able to accept the struggle is part of the journey; after a while, those words become more like whispers of yes and no rather than shouting voices in your head.

I have created a fun exercise for you to download at BookSweetSpot.com. It requires colored pencils and your creative child within you. Get your cape on with the Superhero exercise and create a superhero fitting authentically to your personality, values, and talents.

ENTREPRENEURSHIP AS SUPERHERO

If you think successful entrepreneurs are confident and sure of themselves, I suggest you interview a couple with the purpose of gathering data about the reality of doubt as a grain in the texture of entrepreneurship. You have probably heard of the imposter syndrome. It feels like that. Furthermore, it's easy to get stuck in the struggle where *yes* is the right answer and *no* is the right answer too. The next thing you know, you are sitting on a fence that is rickety and weathered as you stare out at the same field of grass growing.

Although the research literature does not reflect an absolute set of characteristics or set of values, certain recurring themes are associated with entrepreneurial success. The following concepts come from Caliendo and Kritikos:[28]

1. The need to achieve (self-directed and self-efficacy)

2. The desire to have control over one's own destiny (independence and freedom)

3. Stimulation and novelty (risk tolerance, creativity, and openness)

4. Interpersonal reactivity or empathy (optimistic and agreeable)

5. Assertiveness (decisive and persistent)

6. Honesty (integrity and authentic)

Becoming a therapist is considered a calling, and entrepreneurship is considered a calling too. When responding to a calling you are stepping into the role of superhero with your superpowers unique to you. How do you know which way your compass is pointing? Check out your superhero. What is the philosophy of your superhero?

How do you want to define your superhero purpose-driven life, where you are the agent of change in your life and helping others be agents of change in their lives as well? Your purpose and powers are your compass pointing in the direction of how you show up as a therapist and an entrepreneur.

SUMMARY

Throughout history societies have made room for and desired the presence of heroes, from as early as Chiron the wounded healer of Greek mythology to modern contemporary heroes in fantasy and comic books, games, and movies. Superheroes serve a purpose in advancing well-being in cultures from the individual to the group as a whole. As an entrepreneur and therapist you also have a role as a superhero where you will seize the opportunity to fully express and contribute your skills and talents to the community you live in. We need people like you, so get your cape on.

CHAPTER

10

The Foundation—Vision and Mission Statements

Are you ready to breathe life into your dreams and give them form? Your passion, your calling, your life purpose are ready to come to life as a guiding light for your private practice business. Building your business foundation means you will write a vision statement and mission statement. Together, this is the sweet spot from which your business plan flows.

The vision and mission statements reflect your philosophy for your private practice business. Equipped with both, you are in a sweet position to articulate who you are to your peers, potential customers, and clients. The significance of a visible, transparent message is it allows people to know you, like you, and trust you. If you want to take this a step further, you can write a philosophy and a manifesto.

You do not *have to* craft a vision, mission, philosophy, and/or manifesto today. However, I recommend you jot down at least one version of at least a vision and mission statement as a guidepost. Also, if you decide to pursue employment rather than open a private practice, you will have a better chance of getting hired for your dream job. You may find a mission statement comes to you more quickly or a philosophy is straightforward from the heart. Crafting a vision and mission is different for each person, so don't get too hung up on doing this in the right or particular order. Why is this process of crafting a vision, mission, or philosophy important? It is the path to connecting to your ideal client (for more about your ideal client, see Chapter 11). It is also the foundation your practice is built on.

It's important to have a sense of who you enjoy working with while you craft your vision, mission, or philosophy. To avoid paralysis in the process, hold a soft general image of a client you like to work with lightly in your mind—not a death grip. Make the idea of an ideal client a general concept. I encourage you to be mindfully aware of your client image changing or taking shape as you clarify your vision, mission, and philosophy. Sometimes it is easiest if you can think of an actual person you find fulfilling to work with. Let's get to work.

YOUR BLUEPRINT

Remember Sara, the graduate student you met in Chapter 1? Sara participated in one of the first ACT-based coaching groups I facilitated. Her goal was to gain additional skills with the population she felt most passionate about, teens and adults who had been abused as children in their family of origin, before entering private practice. Sara's job search was strategically designed to maximize the chances of gaining valuable experience in this area. She landed her ideal job within a month of graduating.

You, too, have completed enough exercises to design a path for your private practice business. I call the next step the blueprint stage.

Would you build a house without a foundation? Of course not! Then why do people think they can build a successful business without a solid foundation (aka a business plan)? The foundation serves as a 360-degree view of your business. Like a treatment plan, the foundation informs your decisions. No matter what kind of business you build, it needs to sit on top of a solid foundation. There are three essential pieces: your vision, your mission, and your values. All three can be wrapped up into your philosophy. Let's take a look at each concept and its function.

Make notes for yourself as we go along together. Also, you might need to look back at your notes from your previous work. The process of building a foundation is not linear, although I present it step-by-step. So, if you find yourself struggling, go to a different part of the foundation. It is fine to skip around. Just be sure to come back to any section that needs to be fleshed out.

Together, a well-thought-out and well-written vision and mission statement lead to an optimal return on your investment (ROI) of time (your life) and resources (your money). They save you energy and heartache. With the two statements together, you will be able to align people, processes, products, and services toward a successful future. They function to communicate to your potential clients what you offer and how you offer it. Together they are your work persona, not a fake identity.

The *Sweet* SPOT
Private Practice Foundation

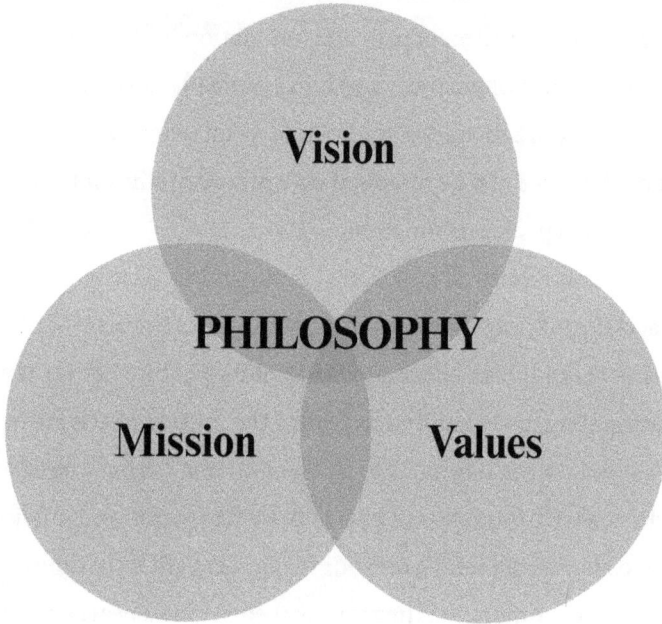

Figure 2: Private Practice Foundation

VISION STATEMENT

A concise **vision** statement makes it easier for people to remember you. Remember the vision board you created in Chapter 8? Your vision board is a good jumping-off point for your vision statement. Naturally, the vision board with its images transcends the limitation of words. Beyond this, the biggest difference between your vision board and a vision statement is the statement is utilized for a consistent message for your marketing collateral: your website, business cards, brochures, elevator speech, networking, social media, and so on. Along with a mission statement, a vision statement is a tool that allows you to know where you are and where you are headed.

What do you want for your private practice business five or ten years from now? When you write your vision statement, pretend you take a trip in a time machine into the future. Take a snapshot of your private practice. What does it look like? What do you see in the future of your private practice business?

A vision statement informs your branding process (covered in detail in Chapter 11). Your vision sustains you when the tasks of your mission seem heavy. Namely, it serves as a "big picture" beyond the day-to-day tasks and makes those tasks meaningful. The vision statement is about the big picture of *what* your private practice (you) hopes to provide. A mission is *how* you will do this.

Check out the following examples of vision statements:

- Alzheimer's Association: Our vision is a world without Alzheimer's disease.

- Avon: To be the company that best understands and satisfies the product, service and self-fulfillment needs of women—globally.

- Norfolk Southern: Be the safest, most customer-focused, and successful transportation company in the world.

- Armstrongs' Counselling Services: To help people transform personal challenges into life-enhancing opportunities.

- Microsoft: Empower people through great software—any time, any place, and on any device.

Your Vision Exercise

It's your turn: What is your vision? Below are two steps to prime the pump. Time to pull your journal out to complete these steps.

Step One

1. Who are you energized to work with? Think about the client(s) you look forward to seeing or talking to each week. Provide a name and a brief description of what it is about them you like. Any specific demographics?

2. When are you invigorated by a client or a problem? Temporal aspects to therapy can be about the therapy hour or about the beginning, middle, or end of therapy.

3. What are their struggles, habits, worries, sorrows, and joys? What are they hoping for in life?

4. What are their roadblocks in life?

5. What is their problem or pain?

Step Two

After reading each question, close your eyes and visualize your client before writing your answer.

1. What is your overarching, big dream for your client?

2. What do you wish for them as you see them and talk with them?

3. How will their life be different or improved?

Your turn to give translating your answers into a vision statement a go. Write a vision statement in your journal.

You're well on your way to building a solid foundation. Congratulations! You have formulated a first draft of your vision statement. Now your future can begin living out on a day-to-day basis.

Your vision statement is your personalized ticket to business success. Read it to yourself and notice how and what you feel in the way of your passion. A clear vision creates the best for all stakeholders: clients, colleagues, referral sources, anyone connected to the success of your private practice business. Feel the inspiration! If you are not satisfied with your first draft, write another. It took me half a dozen revisions to get it right.

Need help? Here is a chance to do some market research. It's not as scary as it sounds.

TEST-DRIVE YOUR VISION

Some of you will find this next step easy, while others might find it challenging. Giving your vision a test drive is your first opportunity at connecting to people who can help you grow your business. A test drive is essentially marketing research. I find this step especially helpful if I'm feeling stuck with finding the right wording. Don't cringe. You can do this.

- It's easy to create a Facebook poll. Post several versions on Facebook and ask for people to choose which they like best. Or if you want to test one version, post it and ask people to interpret what it means to them. Are their answers close to what you imagine for your private practice future?

- Ask family, friends, and colleagues what they think of your vision statement. Let them know it is important for your future success and their honesty is a gift. You can do this via email, text, or face-to-face. If you do face-to-face, have your vision statement written on a 3x5 index card. You can make notes on the back of the card or on a separate 3x5 card. Remember your vision statement is born from your passions and is closely tied to who you are as a person with a purpose in life. You want to be sure you are clearly and concisely communicating your purpose and passion.

With your vision statement well on its way it's time to see how a mission statement plays into building the foundation.

MISSION STATEMENT

Your thoughtful well-written **mission** statement will appeal to and touch the emotions of your potential clients in areas of pain and struggle while providing hope. Remember the vision statement is about the big picture— *what* you hope you will achieve in an overarching dream in your private practice. Your mission is *how* you will accomplish your big picture of your vision.

The mission is the part of the foundation that specifies the materials you will use to finish building your private practice. What is your strategy?

Be easy on yourself. Let's look at a few examples of mission statements to give you ideas:

- Starbucks: To inspire and nurture the human spirit—one person, one cup, and one neighborhood at a time.

- Nike: To bring inspiration and innovation to every athlete in the world.

- Walmart: To help people save money so they can live better. (That's ten words from the biggest retailer on the planet with probably the most complex operation! Compare it to the other mission statements in this list. With a clear, simply stated mission you can tell the world your goal and how you intend to make it happen.)

- Bristol-Myers Squibb: To discover, develop and deliver innovative medicines that help patients prevail over serious diseases.

- Darden Restaurants: To nourish and delight everyone we serve.

- Armstrongs' Counselling Services: To guide and facilitate, while utilizing both traditional and leading-edge therapeutic techniques, an educational and therapeutic experience so clients can acquire:

  - Enhanced self-awareness
  - A clear focus of the issues, problems, patterns, etc.
  - Life-giving tools
  - Resolution of core issues and lifelong patterns of personal struggles
  - The want, the will and the choice to find peace in their lives

I've included Armstrongs' Counselling Services in both vision and mission statement examples. What do you think? Do the mission and vision statement work at clearly stating purpose and how to make purpose happen?

The point is, the mission statement needs to work *for you*. Your clients will get to know you through your vision and mission statements, and then decide if they like you. You do know that not everybody will like you and that is OK, don't you? Are you ready to give it a shot?

As I mentioned earlier, the steps are not necessarily linear. Seldom is a creative process linear. Consequently, sometimes a mission statement is written before the vision statement. Cool. Whatever works for you. A mission statement answers three questions:

- What do you do? What services do you provide (that support your vision)?

- How do you do it? How do you fulfill your vision that is unique to you?

- Whom do you do it for? Describe your client(s).

I encourage people to stay away from the word "help" and the word "client." We like to be people who are capable. There are plenty of words you can use besides "help" that will differentiate you in how you provide that help. If you find yourself writing your vision and mission with the word "help," go back and substitute it with: to assist, to support, to improve, to liberate, to ease, etc. *Help* is bland. You and your clients are dynamic.

I am going to share with you my first written blueprint. I included "purpose" as part of my blueprint.

Purpose
To help people create a life they love living.

Vision
My vision is to offer cutting-edge therapy and coaching services and products that are accessible and sustainable to

individuals, communities, and societies desiring to create rich meaningful lives with integrity, balance, and vitality.

Mission

To help connect people to their values and passions through effective practices and programs which are proven to work. To provide the best available knowledge and skills needed by people so they can be free to choose behaviors that are effective at moving them forward.

Values

To bring to all relationships honesty, integrity, devotion, commitment, and energy in a wholehearted manner with a sense of juicy adventure and gentle compassion that is genuine and authentic.

Let's take a look at Lauren Anderson for another example. Lauren also participated in the first ACT-based coaching group I facilitated. Her first stages of finding clarity included multiple versions of her vision statement. See if you can catch a glimpse of Lauren's passion as she writes about her calling.

I'm a musician and artist turned coach and therapist. I am deeply interested in empowering creative adults to rock their truest selves, helping them say yes to what they want in life, work, love, and friend- ships. As a trained couple and family therapist, I view my clients within the context of their lives, highlighting their strengths rather than labeling them as broken or dysfunctional.

Lauren named her private practice Love & Life Outside the Box. Her vision became her tagline: *Helping creative people create healthy relationships.* She writes:

My mission is to empower creative people to live and love in a way that is authentic…love & life outside the box is about creating a life, friendships, and love relationships that allow you the freedom and courage to be you.

She goes on to write what that includes:

Focusing on:

- healthy boundaries
- accepting yourself and your loved ones
- overcoming the fear of judgment
- freedom from emotional manipulation
- trusting your own opinion
- learning to love and be loved
- creating balance

This is hard work. Your mind might be telling you that you don't need to do this vision and mission crafting. Don't be tempted to skip this step. The warnings about business failures can be averted with a clear and strong vision and mission statement. The hard work begs you to think deeply about how you want to fulfill your purpose and vision in life. It asks you to take a look at yourself and what makes your style and your set of skills and combination of methods unique. Your character, your values, your heart and soul are what will lead you to success. As helpers and healers, we are in the position to guide people to being authentic. With authenticity comes vulnerability. You ask your clients to be brave. You ask your clients to be courageous. You ask your clients to show up. We need to ask the same of ourselves. We need to step into the tough stuff of showing up and taking ownership of the business side of our private practice.

Don't be shy. Claim your passions. As time passes, you will evolve and develop as a private practice business owner and as a therapist. Your vision and mission also mature over time. Are you ready to write your first draft of a mission statement? Put your thoughts in your journal.

My mission is…

TEST-DRIVE YOUR MISSION

Ready for a test drive of your mission statement? Do the same as with your vision statement and put it out there on Facebook. Share it with family, friends, and colleagues. Ask people what they think. How can it be improved? What does it mean to them when they read it?

You will learn something about yourself you did not see before. It takes courage to be vulnerable with market research, even "just" a test drive among friends. Keep an open mind.

See below for what Lauren did for her marketing research. Which one do you like best and least?

Lauren's tagline brainstorm:

1. Helping creative people create healthy relationships

2. Helping creative people create meaningful relationships

3. Helping creative people create authentic relationships

4.   Helping creative people create authentic lives

5.   Helping creative people create authentic lives and relationships

6.   Helping creative people create original lives

7.   Helping creative people create original lives and relationships

8.   Creative people creating original lives

9.   Creative people creating original lives and relationships

I remember the experience of picking names for my children as being exciting and very important to get "right." Why? Because they, my children, were going to have their name for the rest of their lives. My private practice business identity holds a similar level of excitement and pressure. Now I realize good enough vision and mission statements work for a business, especially since your business will evolve and change. Not quite like naming your kiddo, but it can feel as serious. You do want something you can stick with, as being able to stick with your vision is a key to stability. Changing your direction without careful thought will confuse people who are looking for your services. A test drive will help avoid this situation.

CONNECTING VALUES

Values are an integral component of finding your sweet spot. Values connect all the moving parts of your private practice business. I have talked about values already, and you have worked on clarifying yours. Are you ready to embed them into your private practice business plan and identity?

Claiming your values is the easiest piece of a solid foundation. If you have struggled with crafting a satisfactory vision and mission statement, start with a list of your values and work backward to the vision and mission. As I have mentioned, it does not matter how you move through the process as long as you complete a full foundation.

What are your top three to seven values? If you are not able to tell me your chosen values, go back and review the exercises in Chapter 8 and Chapter 9. If you did not download the exercises go to BookSweetSpot.com and complete them now. If you have written vision and mission statements, see if your values are captured within the statements. With clearly stated values, a well-crafted vision statement, and a thoughtful mission statement, you will know how to invest your precious resources of time, money, and energy.

Speaking of investing, let's do an exercise called the Magical Bank.

Magical Bank Exercise

The author of this exercise is unknown, though you may have played this game before. Imagine that you've won the following prize in a contest: Each morning your bank will deposit $86,400 in your private account for your use.

However, this prize has rules, just as any game has certain rules.

The first set of rules:

- Everything you don't spend during each day will be taken away from you.

- You may not transfer money into some other account.

- You may only spend it.

- Each morning upon awakening, the bank deposits into your account another $86,400 for that day.

The second set of rules:

- The bank can end the game without warning; at anytime it can say, "It's over; that's right, the game is over!"

- The bank can close the account and you will not ever receive a new one.

What would you do? You would buy anything and everything you wanted, right?

Not only for yourself, but for all the people you love. Even for people you don't know, because you couldn't possibly spend it all on yourself. You would try to spend every cent and use it all, right? Of course, you would, because you know it would be replenished in the morning, right?

Actually, this game is reality. Are you shocked?

Each of us is already a winner of this prize, and we are in possession of such a magical bank account. We just can't seem to see it.

The prize in the magical bank account is time! Each morning we awaken to receive a prize of 86,400 seconds as a gift of life, and when we go to sleep at night, any remaining time is NOT credited to us.

What we haven't lived up that day is forever lost. Yesterday is forever gone.

Each morning the account is refilled, but the bank can dissolve the account at anytime...without warning.

So, what will *you* do with your 86,400 seconds?

Aren't they worth so much more than the same amount in dollars?

Think about that and always think of this: Enjoy every second of your life, because time races by so much quicker than you think.

"My Values" Exercise

Why choose only three and no more than seven values? So you can spend your Magic Bank of time wisely. Think about it—you have a limited amount of time on this earth. Being spread too thin can lead to burnout. Burnout can lead to business failure. Knowing you are living your values is fulfilling and meaningful. Also, having a reasonable set of values is about self-care. Can you make a list of your values in your journal?

Need an example of how values, vision, and mission can fit together? Journey Mental Health Center in Madison, Wisconsin, is a good example.

MISSION STATEMENT

Improving people's lives by pioneering and sustaining
effective mental health and substance abuse services.

VISION

The vision of Journey Mental Health Center is to become a
center of excellence for the provision of behavioral health
services.

People: Hiring and retaining great employees.

Productivity: Being a model of quality and cost effective
service for other behavioral health organizations.

Partners: Achieving and maintaining the highest levels of
consumer satisfaction.

VALUES
Integrity
Diversity
Respect
Excellence
Accountability
Hope

PHILOSOPHY OR MANIFESTO

If you want, you can take your ideas about vision, mission, and values and roll them into a private practice business philosophy or manifesto. A business philosophy should reflect the leading principles for conducting business. Your stated philosophy ought to energize you and other people, while encapsulating and fleshing out your vision, mission, and values. A manifesto is a strongly stated, inspiring statement of intention that captures your business philosophy and states a plan of action.

The *Sweet* SPOT
Philosophy Components

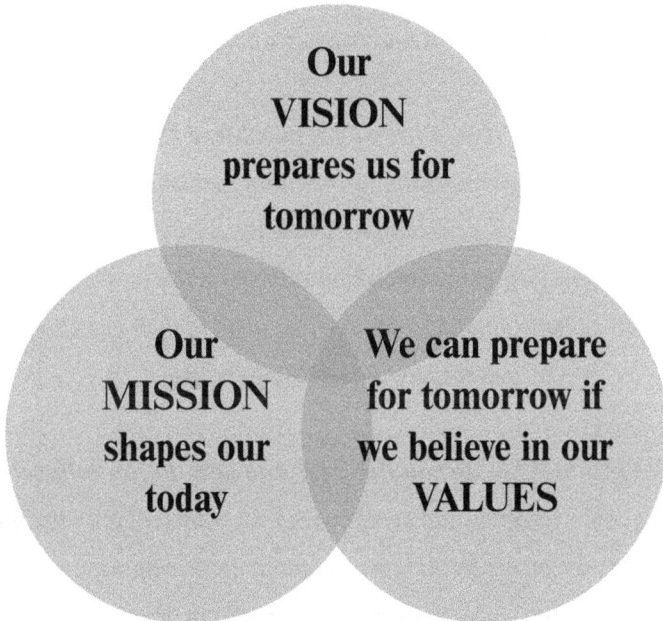

Figure 3: Philosophy Components

Remember Sara, the graduate student? Check out her purpose, vision, and values below.

PURPOSE: *Why do you exist?*

I exist to provide counseling support for people on their healing journey. I exist to provide education to extend the reach of counseling and goodwill toward others.

VISION: *What do you aim to achieve?*
I aim to help people suffering from the effects of abuse, trauma, and grief to heal and to live with more self-compassion, connection to others, and reliance on their inner wisdom.

MISSION: *How do you plan to achieve your vision?*
I plan to achieve my vision by providing group and individual counseling which focuses on authenticity, compassion, balance, and creativity. I envision a counseling practice in which my clients come to embrace themselves and all of their emotions—acceptance empowering change.

VALUES: *What do you stand for and how do you behave?*
I stand for integrity and acceptance. I work toward growth and equality for all people. It is important to me to empower women and children toward lives free from abuse.

POSITIONING: *How do you differentiate yourself from your competition?*
I differentiate myself from my competition because I do not work toward "happy." I believe that therapy, life, in fact, is a journey of acceptance and appreciation for the full range of our emotions, important in leading a balanced and more fulfilled life.

You might be wondering why all this is so important in attracting clients. Can we agree that clients are consumers? Yep, consumers of mental health services. The marketplace has moved away from considering people who go to a therapist for counseling as *patients*. Sometimes people don't even like to consider themselves as mental health clients—it doesn't feel right. Stigma is still sticky.

In today's world, thanks to the internet, consumers of mental health services are more informed and savvier than ever. They have educated themselves. Because of the higher level of knowledge available through blogs, online newsletters, YouTube, and other social media platforms, people get to know you before they ever contact you for an appointment. They research what ails them. Often by the time they contact you, they have a self-ascribed diagnosis for their situation. That being said, people call you with the intention to acquire your services based on three criteria: 1) know you, 2) like you, and 3) trust you. How and what you communicate need to be consistent and authentic. You probably learned through your training that people prefer predictability. It is a topic often highlighted in parenting training and articles. A solid foundation for a private practice business is a clear identity with a consistent message to the people in your community and in your marketplace—and your vision, mission, and values provide that foundation.

SUMMARY

Your private practice identity is closely linked to your personal identity. The three core elements that make up those identities are values, vision, and mission. Ideally they are well crafted and articulated for the purpose of guiding your financial decisions, marketing strategies, and time management processes. You can flesh out these three elements and develop a philosophy with guiding principles for how you conduct your private practice business. You also have a choice to compose a manifesto. Together or alone, these support you and inform every level of future growth in your private practice business.

Your foundation is intimately related to your niche and your brand. Remember your brand is just another label taken from the business lexicon to refer to your identity. Same bird, different feathers. Next let's look at niche and brand in closer detail.

CHAPTER

11

Branding: Hat Racks and Anchors

You have looked backward, you have looked forward, and you have looked inside. You have percolated, and you have filtered through your dreams from multiple perspectives. Does it feel like you are at your sweet spot? Some of the final touches in this section are about up-leveling your sweet spot with fun things like colors, a logo, signatures, and communication style. You are going to create a tagline and an elevator speech that become your signature and go with you wherever you go, be it online or in person.

Even when you are sleeping, your brand will be working hard for you, connecting to your ideal client, your niche, and your target market. It is very possible your brand will also reach people beyond your niche, because you and your private practice are memorable. In this fast-paced, complicated, information-laden culture, you need to give people a hat rack to hang their recall on because of all the noise we have to cut through.

MAKE IT MEMORABLE

The human organism is made to retain all it learns. Otherwise our ABCs and 123s would escape us, and we would have to keep learning the same old thing over and over every day. Our learning history does not evaporate. Our whole organism is a system where we can keep adding more—we are an additive learning system. Keep pouring more into us. We learn with our whole body. It's amazing. Sometimes we have so much in our organism it gets lost if we are not in close proximity and using it on a regular basis. However, it is not gone.

What do recall, remembering, and retrieval have to do with branding? Informational overload makes it harder for people to remember you and your private practice. Then they need to be able to remember what you actually do. You're smart, so I think you get the idea of where we are headed. Let's make you unforgettable!

Here is a cool tidbit about branding if you are experiencing some resistance to the idea: Effective branding of mental health conditions breaks down the stigma associated with using your services.[29] The results are an increase in consumers' willingness to access mental health services. Branding helps create an emotional connection with your niche and builds a sense of community. Cool, huh? Although I am talking about branding as a marketing tool, branding is a style of communication using words, images, symbols, and colors to begin a conversation with your potential client. Think of branding as relationship-building. Meanwhile, familiarize yourself with some business lingo you need to know as we move forward.

- **Target market** refers to the people who are most likely to buy your services. This is a broad group. Consumers of mental health services or coaching are one target market. The people (consumers) in the target market are generally identified demographically.

- **Demographics** are characteristics of a population, such as age, gender, relationship status, educational level, income, etc.

- **Market segmentation** refers to how the target market is divided into groups and subgroups based on similar characteristics. This can be accomplished by separating segments out by demographics or segmenting through psychographics (see below). A segmentation of the mental health consumer target market might be divided as follows (each can be a standalone segment or combined): 1) women, 2) over the age of forty, 3) single, 4) college-educated, and 4) working full-time.

- **Niche** is an even smaller subset of the target market segmentation, with particular needs, wants, and preferences unique to the group. Piggybacking on the example above, a niche might look like this: *Serving single women over the age of forty with a post-graduate degree in the STEM field who live in New York City and are looking for dating and relationship guidance.* A niche is easier to talk with as a small group using their language. The danger of a niche is if it is *too* small, such as *single women between the ages of forty and fifty who live in upstate New York.* You can hone in on demographic and psychographic descriptors to identify your niche.

- **Persona** is a description of your **ideal client**—who they are and how they use your services. The persona of your ideal client serves as an imaginary person you talk to when you create your marketing messages.

- **Psychographics** is the study of attitudes, aspirations, and other psychological criteria that make up your niche. These include personality, values, lifestyle choices, and beliefs.

- **Brand** is a term I use throughout *Sweet Spot*. But what exactly is a brand? It is everything about you and your private practice: what you promise to your clients, their perception of who you are, and what they expect from you. It is your business persona. It incorporates the five senses into a consistent experience—visual, auditory, tactile, olfactory, and taste.

  - Visual: colors, logo, shape, signatures—all communicate a message.
  - Auditory: whatever people hear such as videos, a pitch or elevator speech, or music on your website or blog.
  - Tactile: business cards, furniture, brochures.
  - Olfactory (smell): essential oils or aromatherapy.
  - Taste: candy in the office or at networking events.

Armed with the knowledge of what a brand is and what it implies allows you to unlock the power of a unique selling proposition, also referred to as a unique selling point (USP). Plus, you are equipped to genuinely speak to your potential ideal clients about the benefits they receive when they work with you. It's a win-win situation for you and the people you serve.

Yes, your brand is you; you are your brand. You might be saying to yourself, *I am not a brand.* True. That being said, I can promise you people will brand you, as we are all prone to stereotyping, categorizing, and sorting behaviors to simplify life. People will distinguish you from the therapist down the street by who you are and what you do. The exercises in this section pave the way for you to be purposeful and intentional in your branding so you can establish a viable position in the marketplace.

IDEAL CLIENT

Let's get down to business and figure out who fits into your target market. When you think of your ideal client, think in terms of archetypes. An archetype is a broad identity, such as outgoing, or nerdy, or introverted. Most of us have heard of Myers-Briggs personality types, and it's a great place to cull ideas from about archetypes. There is a ton of information online about Myers-Briggs; I like the website 16 Personalities—plus they offer a free test (*www.16personalities.com/free-personality-test*).

With an archetype in mind, you develop a dialogue about what you offer in the way of services and the benefits clients receive when they work with you. You are attuned to and in alliance with them (see Chapter 12 for more on attunement and alliance). You know you offer the best of your therapeutic self to them in a way that is aligned with your integrity. There is no "one" cookie-cutter client profile that fits into your target market. As mentioned in the business vocabulary list above, your target market is made up of individuals who share commonalities across a broad spectrum of life circumstances. When a potential client begins looking for services, they are most likely in pain or struggling with being stuck in an uncomfortable spot in life.

If you let fear be the motivator of your marketing and branding choices, you might be tempted to say you can work with anyone and everyone. Your fear of not having enough clients can dilute the conversation with your potential client, and you could end up with fewer clients or pricing your services too low and developing burnout. It is not unusual to experience fear in defining your niche, because your mind will tell you that you'll miss out on an opportunity. However, common sense tells us there is no way we are meant to work with everybody. We simply cannot be everything to everyone. Would you agree? In this case it is best for you and your client to fit together reasonably well.

The people you look forward to working with in private practice have a script they carry in their head about life, problems, solutions, and so on. You can pick their brains with a brief interview. Choose three to five people you think fit the category of a possible client. The interviewees must be people you like to be around, and they can include children and adolescents. They can be a family member, friend, colleague, or an acquaintance you enjoy. You can include previous clients, if you want. If you want to work with couples and families, an ideal client interview might be more challenging, so I recommend you interview the person who will be driving the inquiry. It is best if you pick from different relational categories. Don't interview all your family members. Mix it up with family, friends, and acquaintances.

Ideal Client Interview Exercise

Write the names of your interviewees in your journal before reading any further. Take a few minutes to do this, as it is important for the second half of this exercise.

It is best if you can talk to the person face-to-face or on the phone. Don't just send a bunch of questions for them to write answers to because that gives them too much time to script an answer. As you conduct the interviews, take notes on specific words they use, especially if the word seems to hold a strong charge. Just as in the therapy room, we enter the client's world by using their language. When you use the language of the speaker, you are being *attuned* with them.

First, let's gather a few basic demographics. You will want to make up an interview form for each interviewee to record your notes. This is similar to an intake. Most of us have been trained to take a client history or, at the minimum, gather basic information about the client. Use this as a model to create an interview form for each person on your list.

Demographic information categories need to be worded to be culturally sensitive. You can throw in some geographic information too. Where your client lives can say a lot about them—consider country club, urban or rural area, and so on.

- Age
- Gender
- Ethnicity
- Household income (I have a difficult time asking this one)
- Relationship status
- Education
- Professional status

Once you have gathered demographic information, you will explore four major life domains during your interviews. The Sweet Spot Bullseye is a useful form for this part of the interview (see Figure 4, below). I like the Bullseye, as it yields an abundance of information. When people miss the center in the domains, they experience frustration, anger, depression, anxiety, and so on, and will search out solutions to their problems or try to gain control of their uncomfortable feelings. They will look for someone who speaks their language and offers an understanding of their situation.

Below is a description of each of the four domains and a set of questions for you to ask your volunteer potential client. Customize the interview questions for each individual. You want to probe with open-ended questions. Use your therapy skills and practice your mindfulness skills by noticing what resonates with your interviewee and with you. Read the definition of each domain to each person first, to be sure you're both on the same page. Also, listen carefully to the vocabulary they use. These are words you can use to market yourself. After you are finished, you can ask them where they would put themselves on the Bullseye.

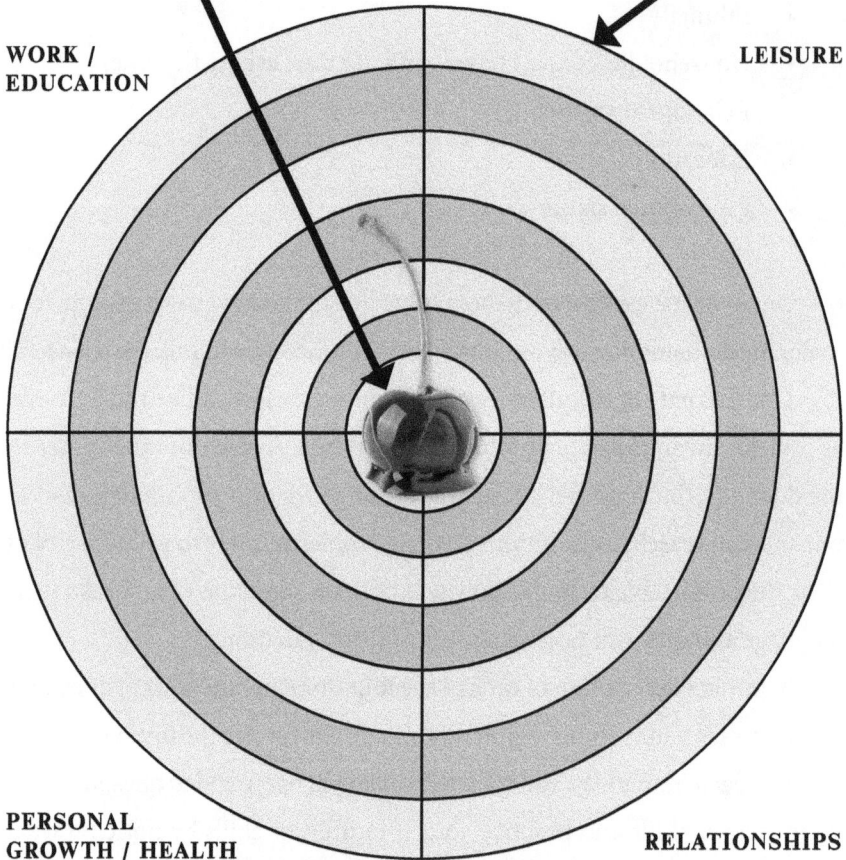

I am living fully by my values

I am acting very inconsistent with my values

WORK / EDUCATION

LEISURE

PERSONAL GROWTH / HEALTH

RELATIONSHIPS

The Bullseye *Sweet* SPOT

Figure 4: The Sweet Spot Bullseye.
Based on Tobias Lundgren's 'Bull's Eye' exercise

FOUR MAJOR LIFE DOMAINS

When you create your interview form, leave plenty of room to write the answers.

1. **Work/Education**: *refers to your workplace and career, education and knowledge, and skills development. This may include volunteering and other forms of unpaid work.*

    Ask for specifics with those great therapy questions you know how to ask. Probe: "Tell me more?" "And..." is a good word to utter with a pause to encourage them to keep talking.

    *   What seems most important to you about your work, career, and education/training?
    *   What is going well for you with work, career, or education/training?
    *   What's your biggest frustration with work, career, or education/training?
    *   What are your aspirations for work, career, or education/training?
    *   Is there anything I missed or you want to add?

2. **Leisure:** *refers to how you play, relax, stimulate, or enjoy yourself, including your hobbies or other activities for rest, recreation, fun, and creativity.*

    Ask probing questions.

    *   What seems most central to you about the domain of leisure?
    *   What is going well for you with the different aspects of this domain in your life?
    *   What's your biggest disappointment about your leisure?
    *   What are your wishes for leisure in your life?
    *   Is there anything I missed or you want to add?

3. **Relationships**: *refers to intimacy, closeness, friendship, and bonding. This includes relationships with your partner, children, parents, relatives, friends, coworkers, and other social contacts.*

    - What seems most important to you about the different relationships in your life? (As a reminder, ask for specifics with those great therapy questions you know how to ask. Probe.)
    - What is going well for you with the different relationships in your life?
    - What's your biggest disturbance with the different relationships in your life?
    - What are your desires for the different relationships in your life?
    - Is there anything I missed or you want to add?

    Personal Growth/Health: *refers to your ongoing development as a human being. This may include organized religion, personal expressions of spirituality, creativity, developing life skills, meditation, yoga, getting out into nature, exercise, nutrition, and addressing health.*

    Probe with curiosity.

    - What seems most vital to you about this domain in your life?
    - What is going smoothly for you with the different aspects of this domain in your life?
    - What's your biggest challenge with the ongoing processes of personal growth and health?
    - What wishes do you hold as important to you in this domain of your life?
    - Is there anything I missed or you want to add?

In case you need or want more information, here are a few more areas you can formulate questions for, for a full psychographic picture. This is meaty stuff, so don't skip it:

Personality

(Outgoing, quiet, Myers-Briggs, Enneagram, Type A)

Attitudes about

(Money, politics, religion, etc.)

Interested in

(What holds their attention? E.g., Music, radio, hobbies, activities, magazines, blogs, habits.)

Example questions:

- Where do you get your information about what is happening in your family, neighborhood, community, and the world?

- What programs do you watch on TV, listen to on the radio, follow on social media, etc.? (Get specific details such as the name of blogs or magazines they read.)

- Do you have favorite stores (brick-and-mortar or online) for shopping? What do you like about them?

- What does a typical day look like?

- Ask about favorite movies, books, and quotes.

INFORMATION HELPS YOU HELP THEM

You might be wondering how gathering this information helps you help your client. Answer: this information is the first step in building rapport and increases your comfort level with the voice you use in your marketing collateral. (We will look more closely at building rapport in Chapter 12.) It's easy to conclude that when we know ourselves and our potential clients, and can speak their language, it will lead to a better fit. You can be authentic, and they will experience your authenticity. People make decisions based on emotions, and if they feel like you understand them, you are better able to make a connection.

By this point you should have a clear profile of your target market, your market segment, your niche, and your ideal client. If not, do this: Go through the back door. Make a list of who or what you do *not* want to work with. Case in point, I do not want to work with addictions, so I refer potential clients to other colleagues who thrive working with addictions. Nor do I want to work with train-wrecked couples. Again, I refer them to other colleagues who are passionate about these issues. It's just as important to know who you do not want to work with as who you do. Your discomfort may be another colleague's ideal client.

HAT RACKS AND ANCHORS

Before we get going on taglines and elevator speeches, let's be curious about the function of each. The question of *workability* lies at the heart of ACT.

In the spirit of workability, an elevator speech and a tagline are communication tools. Together they are considered a **pitch**. Your pitch is the *hat rack* for people to hang their hat on, so they know where to find you when they need your services or to refer someone to.

A hat rack is a fairly simple piece of construction. It is a rack with a few posts sticking out where you can rest your hat then retrieve it when you are ready to wear it again. Simple is the secret to crafting an elevator speech and tagline. Retrieval is key for people to recall and remember you. You are your brand. I'm not saying you are like a product for trade like a box of soap, but I am suggesting who you are as a person is the "what" that attracts or repels people.

Your tagline and elevator speech help you to be memorable and stand out in the crowd. Being consistent and memorable in your pitch allows people in your target market and niche to identify with you as the person who "gets" them. You not only speak their language, but you understand their pain and can help. Ideally, this creates a mutually good fit. Your elevator speech should communicate to others your talents and gifts (those parts of your transcendent self) that are of service to them and will help them realize their fullest potential.

Your pitch helps you be in alignment with yourself. Most of us suffer from some anxiety when we go to networking events (online or live). Having a pitch allows you to *drop anchor*. It helps you make room for being frazzled. It helps you be present without saying too little or too much. A well-crafted pitch is another sweet spot, just like in the story of "Goldilocks and The Three Bears." She finds the pot of porridge that is just right—not too hot and not too cold. An elevator speech is the same.

More than once when attending a training or workshop at a national convention, I forgot to drop anchor and poof! I turned into a wallflower. I stood back and listened without uttering much more than my name. I have a tendency to be withdrawn when I encounter people I perceive as smarter or more experienced than I am. We all have one or two of those kinds of stories. As a wallflower, I noticed people who were talking who went on and on and on about who they were and what they did. They did it all and worked with everybody. I figured they were coping with nervousness in the opposite manner as I was, by talking endlessly but it seemed to be without a purpose—at least, not a purpose I could discern. Their professional identity/ brand was muddled with too much information. Once I connected with my elevator speech, I was able to focus on my passion rather than my nervousness and could drop anchor with a short introduction.

Here is a challenge for you. The next time you are at a personal or professional gathering with strangers, listen. Listen closely to other people. Take time to notice when your attention starts to drop off and wander. Notice what your mind holds onto about the person speaking, especially after the gathering is over. Who do you remember? What do you remember? What sticks with you? The secret to developing an elevator speech and a tagline that communicate you, your brand, is to be simple—that is what makes it sticky.

YOUR ELEVATOR SPEECH

The ideal length of an elevator speech is sixty to ninety seconds. You state a problem in the first few words, offer up a solution next, and tell what makes you different—all while knowing you are talking to or about your ideal client.

My first elevator speech:

> I work with *adult survivors* (target market) of *catastrophic violence* (problem) who want to *create a life beyond loss and trauma* (solution) by teaching them how to make effective decisions with *proven strategies* (my USP), so they can live a life that is *meaningful and fulfilling* (benefits of working with me).

People are curious and will ask me questions about how I work. Then I tell a story about success with a client. Storytelling is a skill you can acquire that helps you be relatable and memorable. Be interesting if you are going to use storytelling as a communication skill to connect. The purpose of having a story is to add flesh to the sixty-second elevator speech.

Getting Started on Your Elevator Speech Exercise

You can write the answers to the below questions in your journal, or download the Elevator Speech and Tagline worksheet from BookSweetSpot.com.

Part 1: Spend some time writing answers to the following questions.

1. Who you do want to work with (your target audience/niche)? State this using words other than "client" or a label such as "borderline." You work with people: kids, teens, families, couples. What is their pain?

2. What value do you provide in connection to their problem (your solution)?

3. How do you do it uniquely (this is your USP or unique selling point)?

Here is a longer version of my elevator speech:

My name is Brenda Bomgardner, and I love supporting adult survivors of catastrophic violence, such as childhood physical and sexual abuse, neglect, and abandonment, as they move beyond the wounds of trauma and loss. I am fiercely committed to assisting people discover how to live a vibrant and meaningful life by teaching them how to make effective decisions with proven methods based on evidence-based strategies. Again, my name is Brenda Bomgardner.

Always repeat your name, as listeners have a tendency to forget. It makes a good first impression. A stranger you meet for the first time will form a first impression within the first sixty seconds of meeting you. Hence, no sense in rambling on.

Part 2: Construct your elevator speech.

Following are the components of the elevator speech:

1. Begin with your name.

2. State who you want to work with and their problem. In marketing lingo, their pain point.

3. State your passion about the solution you offer.

4. State the benefit(s) of working with you.

5. Say how you do what you do.

You can have a call to action here too. For example: *I am accepting new clients. Please feel free to pick up a brochure and leave me your contact information.*

The first step is to write it out. The second is to rehearse it. Rehearse it in front of the mirror, driving in the car, or while cooking dinner. You may notice your elevator speech comes out different each time. No problem. The idea is to get comfortable publicly stating who you are, what you do, who you work with, and the problem you solve. A big tidbit about ACT is we don't focus on solving the problem of symptoms, we solve the problem of being entangled with problem-solving behavior, and this is done by changing your relationship with unnecessary suffering. Know what you do and how you do it.

TAGLINE

A tagline is a shorter version of your elevator speech that you can include on your printed material such as brochures, business cards, flyers, your website, and so on. Like an elevator speech, a tagline is simple and memorable. And yes, again, it's part of your branding. A tagline has a lasting effect and appeals to a person's emotions by stating the benefits. Like *Get Your*

Happiness On. Mine was *Create a Life You Love Living.* Think of your tagline as a headline for your private practice. Nobody is going to refer to you because you have a tagline—it is meant to encourage curiosity so the reader will want to learn more about you.

Are you beginning to see the usefulness of developing marketing messages? Can you see how your brand becomes a hat rack and an anchor? It can hold you steady. It allows for a sense of security to develop for you and for others. I find comfort in this process. See what you notice as you go through these steps yourself.

BRANDING IS ABOUT RELATIONSHIP

Essentially, branding is about the relationship among you and people in your niche. We are again touching on therapeutic skills that work in the realm of marketing your private practice. The relationship is realized through a skill called perspective-taking: an awareness that others have different thoughts, emotions, reactions, intentions, experiences, and beliefs than we do, and that we can experience ourselves through empathy.

Your brand is communicated through your demeanor, your choice of words, and your personality, as I mentioned before. It is the distillation of who you are and how others experience you. I describe brand as a full sensory experience, from the colors you use, your stationery, the sound of your voice on your message machine or vlog. It is the felt sense people have when they come in contact with any aspect of you and your practice. It's your energy. It's the cadence in your voice. It is the soul of who you are from the inside out. It is difficult to capture a brand in just words, although words are necessary to get your message across in a consistent and reliable manner that reflects your professional identity. Everything you say, do, and use as marketing collateral is relationship building. I see it as courtship.

SUMMARY

Your brand functions as a hat rack for your niche and an anchor for you in rough waters. Your brand is an integral part of your business plan and will help you stand out in a competitive marketplace. I have brought into focus crossover therapy skills to build a relationship with someone you have not yet met, your ideal client. Knowing how to identify your ideal client within your niche is accomplished with questions about demographics, psychographics, and demographics. All this is rounded out with an elevator speech and a tagline, your pitch. You're ready to move on to an even sweeter spot: Three A's and how they relate to your niche.

CHAPTER

12

Attunement, Alignment, and Alliance

The Three A's of an effective therapeutic relationship are attunement, alignment, and alliance. When the Three A's are present, the prognosis for desirable therapeutic outcomes is high. These are skills honed throughout school, internships, workshops, and professional training. Maybe you are a natural at the Three A's and developed these three skills before you started your formal training. This is great news for you as a business owner. Listen up! Your Three A's skills are transferable business skills and will guide you to a great-fitting niche.

Many therapists cringe when they think of marketing, as if marketing is a dirty word or some kind of dirty deed. Marketing is not an evil, deceptive endeavor. Word of mouth is a form of marketing, and do you think that is bad? Of course, you don't. It is the best marketing you or I can have. Word of mouth occurs when you provide high-quality therapy and make a commitment to deliver the best standard of care possible to each and every one of your clients. This is accomplished with awareness and present-moment mindfulness skills. I can attest this is easier to do when you and your client are a good fit.

Your Three A's skills come into play as you build trust and develop a safe rapport with your clients. Simply put, clients are your target market. If that sounds odd, it is because you don't relate to your clients as target markets. We don't want to lose sight of the fact that our target market and niche are made up of people. Occasionally, when using business and marketing terms, the people factor becomes obscured—much like when we use jargon to talk about symptoms and diagnoses. We treat people; we don't treat the diagnosis. Same for marketing: we work with people, not target markets. It boils down to the reality that all business is a person-to-person endeavor.

We are going to build on the branding work from Chapter 11. The identity of your ideal client should be taking shape within a clearly defined niche. You are going to use your AAA skills and natural gifts to grow your relationship with your ideal client. That's right—your therapy skills will help you grow your business with a solid client base. You may not know it now, but the therapist in you is also a natural marketer.

Let's start with attunement.

ATTUNEMENT

Attunement is your ability to be fully present with your client and pick up on the nuances of their communication. Attunement is your ability to let them know you see, hear, and feel *with* them beyond empathy and beyond active listening, and that you are "tuned in" on multiple levels. Your clients sense when you accurately perceive them and what they are experiencing. Attunement also contains an element of curiosity. A popular image of attunement is the gaze between an infant and mother or father. It is a felt experience. In his book *To Sell Is Human*, Daniel Pink says attunement is the ability to bring your actions and outlook into harmony with other people and within the context you're in.[30] How do you begin to create this experience with your potential client? How can you be present with someone you have never met? This is accomplished with an accurate portrayal of who you are and who your ideal client is through your marketing collateral.

Looking at trust from the lens of the business world is similar to the lens of the therapy world. In the business world, "interpersonal reactivity" is a term used to describe the entrepreneurial qualities of being empathic, optimistic, and agreeable. Other studies indicate emotional stability, calmness, and being robust are the qualities or skills that add to enhanced performance of entrepreneurial success.[31] Your therapy skill of attunement encompasses many of these qualities. Your ability to be with another person as if you were in their skin allows you to connect. This is particularly important to the success of your private practice business.

ALIGNMENT

Next is **alignment**. It is intertwined with attunement and alliance. Alignment is more about your internal workings and how you let others know you. Qualities of alignment include being true to who you are as a person of integrity. I call alignment being in a position of high fidelity with your intentions and knowing what those intentions are. You have a responsibility to yourself to do the best you can. It is not about being the best or knowing you are the best. Take perfection out of the equation. It's more about the confidence you have in yourself, knowing you will be the best you can be at any given time.

You are human, and it is human to have off days and still do the best you can. When you are up late with a loved one who is sick or suffering, and you still go to work and do the best you can with your clients, you are acting in high fidelity. You are in alignment. Another way to look at alignment is to know you are an integrated individual. Just as with attunement, people notice when you are in alignment with yourself.

ALLIANCE

Finally, we have **alliance**. Whether you are a newly minted therapist or a seasoned one, you probably understand the need for a collaborative, safe relationship that fosters the growth of trust. As I mentioned earlier, trust is the bedrock of the therapeutic alliance—and marketing. Trust is formed collaboratively. Together the two of you will form a bond.

Being trustworthy is an earned quality in almost all relationships. Not everybody is easily won over just because you say, "Trust me." You need to demonstrate you are trustworthy. How? Imagine your potential client is ready to change and face a difficult situation. They have reached a point and are ready to step into the unknown, hoping one of two things will happen: they will know how to fly, or there will be solid ground to stand on. You embody both. What is important is that you are willing to be both. You are committed to being the safety net as well as the wings in a collaborative, respectful manner, and you are willing to step into the darkness with them. You have their best interest at heart. Does this sound like you? Absolutely, it does.

MARKETING FUNNEL

Now that you understand the Three A's, let's talk about how they relate to your target market and creating a marketing funnel. *What the heck is a marketing funnel?* you might ask. It is a simple process your potential clients will move through before making an appointment; it's sometimes referred to as the sales or buying cycle. The four steps in the process are: Know me.

Like me. Trust me. Use me. The first three steps lead to a position or process of closing the deal (the Use Me fourth step).

Potential clients will contact you for an appointment only if they believe they can trust you, and they have experienced a trigger to call you for therapy when they want to buy your services. I know when I was first exposed to the concept that clients *buy* mental health services, it felt foreign. In the business world, however, that is what it is. And when your potential ideal client calls and you hope you are a good fit, you will want to close the deal. Although this language sounds rather coldhearted, I want you to understand the business concepts because these business concepts will help you make wise ethical decisions. The object of closing the deal is to be confident you can be of service to your client. You don't want to close the deal with someone who is a poor fit. You don't want to close the deal with a client who needs services beyond your expertise. Both are bad business decisions and may border on unethical.

Before a person enters the marketing funnel, they enter into the buying cycle in the following progression. As I take you through the marketing funnel, see how Figure 5 below fits, and how and when the Three A's come to play a part. I suspect they are present from the very beginning. The buying cycle looks a lot like the stages of change in Motivational Interviewing. But, hey, you decide.

The marketing funnel: Know me, like me, trust me…use me (close the deal).

The *Sweet* SPOT *Buying Cycle*

MOTIVATIONAL INTERVIEWING STAGES OF CHANGE		MARKETING FUNNEL

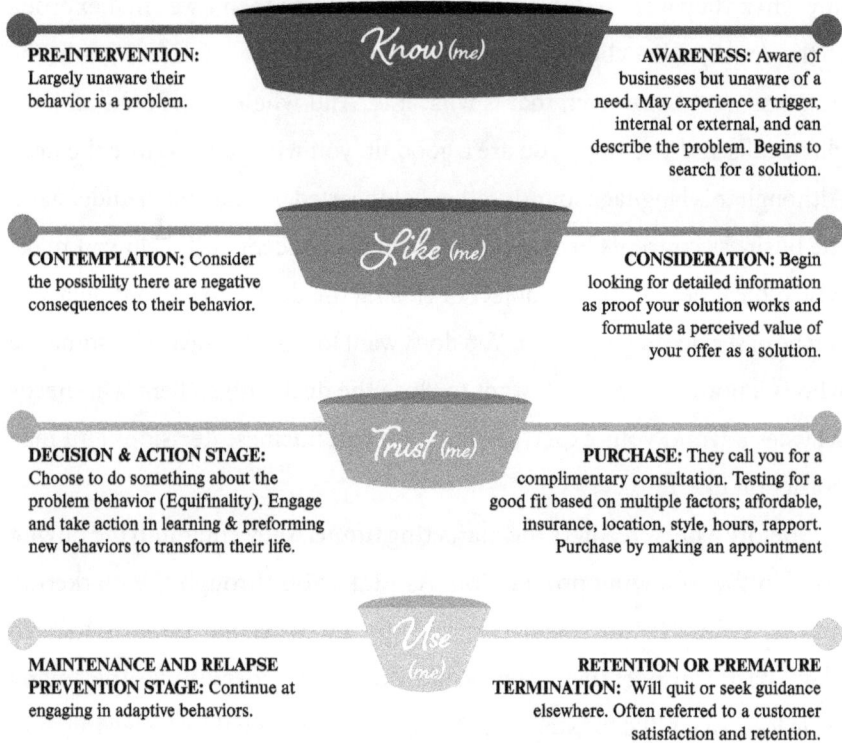

PRE-INTERVENTION: Largely unaware their behavior is a problem.

Know (me)

AWARENESS: Aware of businesses but unaware of a need. May experience a trigger, internal or external, and can describe the problem. Begins to search for a solution.

CONTEMPLATION: Consider the possibility there are negative consequences to their behavior.

Like (me)

CONSIDERATION: Begin looking for detailed information as proof your solution works and formulate a perceived value of your offer as a solution.

DECISION & ACTION STAGE: Choose to do something about the problem behavior (Equifinality). Engage and take action in learning & preforming new behaviors to transform their life.

Trust (me)

PURCHASE: They call you for a complimentary consultation. Testing for a good fit based on multiple factors; affordable, insurance, location, style, hours, rapport. Purchase by making an appointment

MAINTENANCE AND RELAPSE PREVENTION STAGE: Continue at engaging in adaptive behaviors.

Use (me)

RETENTION OR PREMATURE TERMINATION: Will quit or seek guidance elsewhere. Often referred to a customer satisfaction and retention.

Figure 5: The Sweet Spot Buying Cycle

Know Me: *Awareness*

The first step in the marketing funnel, *know me*, is when a potential client becomes aware of you and your services. Your potential client might find you through an online directory, a Google search, or maybe a referral from a colleague or doctor. Perhaps a family member or friend suggests you. Even if a former client refers the potential client to you, the potential client will move through the same steps in the marketing funnel. The individual differences are how quickly they move through the funnel and what eventually triggers them to pick up the phone and call you for an appointment. Some people take longer, while others move pretty quickly.

A prospective client needs to experience a trigger similar to those talked about in the therapy room. The best way to understand triggers is that something happens in the person's environment that prompts the person to search for a solution—you, other therapists, or other alternatives solutions are available as possible solutions. This solution-seeking behavior is often described as your client's "pain point." Within ACT, a pain point can be seen as behavior that moves a person away (escape) from discomfort or moves a person toward (satisfaction) a desired, valued situation. Most of the time the motivation to seek therapy is a combination of both escape and satisfaction. Either way, you know their pain from both sides, away and toward. You appeal to them because you have done your homework and have a good idea of who this person is. One final piece of this first step is the person needs to be aware of you, and this is accomplished—you guessed it—through marketing.

Like Me: Consideration

The next step in the funnel, *like me*, is when a potential client checks you out through your website or blog. Maybe they look you up on LinkedIn or some other social media platform. All they have to do is Google your name. Count on it; they will carry out some type of detective work to see if you are a person they might like. What makes you likable is your ability to understand them and convey that understanding to them, *and* your solution. However, clients don't instantly call (like) you. Just like in real life, it takes a while to know you.

You have the opportunity to build rapport through your marketing efforts. A buying trigger might happen at this step if they perceive you as the "one." If a person contacts you here, it is not a guarantee they are ready to use you for your talented therapy skills; they might be interviewing others. So, it is good to get your Three A's on when they contact you.

Trust Me: Purchase

If you are likable, the third step, *trust me*, begins. Only when your potential client trusts you will they move to the purchase stage (use me). This could be very quick, so it might seem as if *like me* and *trust me* happen together. But they are distinct. Think about it; don't take my word for it. Even a product such as McDonald's is built on trust. You can trust you will have the same-tasting burger each and every time and at any location at any time of day. They are predictable. Remember, predictable is the cornerstone of trust, security, good parenting, and stable relationships. Thanks to the internet, your potential client is out there trying to find an ideal fit with a mental health service provider or coach to help them with their problems. They are in pain, and they want someone just right for them. This is where the Three A's come in to help you be the "just right" provider for them.

The four components of trust are benevolence, integrity, competence, and predictability. The Three A's are how we communicate trust. Research on trustworthiness indicates people decide if you look trustworthy from a photo within one hundred milliseconds.[32] This tells me a good photo is a necessity, and it should match your marketing messages.

Defusion Exercise

I want to check in with you about your thoughts on marketing and the whole idea of a marketing funnel. Is your mind saying: *Wait a minute. I don't need to do this marketing stuff. I can just hang my shingle and they will come?* Trust me. That works, but it takes a long time.

The mind is excellent at keeping you safe, so it's going to try and talk you out of taking a risk that leaves you feeling vulnerable. I say this because marketing is a vulnerable endeavor. You become more publicly visible. It's not like therapy, which happens behind closed doors and is private.

You may be an excellent practitioner and believe that is enough to build your private practice business. Some people choose to go the insurance route rather than market a private pay practice. If that works for you, then go for it. It's still a form of marketing, however. Through the years I have heard, "I don't like marketing. I don't think marketing is honest. I don't like exposing myself. I hate rejection." What if I told you that you can have those thoughts and still move forward? The questions remain: *Is having your own private practice worth it? Is it worth taking the risk to be seen?*

Once you use a defusion skill, and there are many ways to learn defusion, you have an increased opportunity to follow through with behaviors that are in alignment with your value-guided goals. The *follow-through behavior* is referred to as *mood-independent behavior*. Holy cow! You do this all the time. Have you ever been in a mood to sleep in and not go to work or class, and you managed to get yourself out of bed and went to work or class anyway? You know how to do this thing called mood-independent behavior. Defusion skills do not "fix" the feelings. Defusion skills provide space and time to connect and act.

Remember the defusion exercise in Chapter 5 (Preparedness)? Let's practice it again. *I am having the thought* is one of my favorite defusion techniques. It was originally called the "deliteralization of language" or "cognitive deliteralization." You don't have to take your thoughts as literal truths or facts. You can have your thoughts and still act in a way that moves you toward a highly valued action toward accomplishing a goal. The script is used again here with different wording. First read the whole exercise, then go back and complete each step, paying attention to what happens.

Say to yourself:

1. *I am having the thought that I hate marketing.* Say it **three** more times with your eyes closed.

2. Now say, *I am **noticing** I am having the thought that I hate market-ing*. Say it **three more** times with your eyes closed.

3. Now say, *I am noticing that I am noticing that I am having the thought that I hate marketing*. You got it—close your eyes and repeat it **three** times.

What were your observations? The more you practice the better you get at creating space for your thoughts, urges, emotions, and sensations, and acting in alignment with your values.

This is a mindfulness defusion exercise designed to help you be open to experiencing your thoughts, feelings, and emotions and still move toward your dream. I am asking you a serious question. Is this what you wish for your clients? Do you hope they can take action to live a life based on what is important to them even when scared or unsure?

I tell the people I work with they already have the skill and name it for them. I already mentioned work as a skill; how about exercise? Mood-independent behavior? Can you name a few more? Mood-independent behavior allows you and your clients to further develop the skills for having a self-directed life. Also, one of the most appealing reasons people become entrepreneurs and business owners is their desire to be in control of their destiny. You are the agent of change. I know you became a therapist to help people. You can be a helper *and* you can be a business owner.

When you communicate the Three A's effectively, you will increase the probability of attracting your ideal client. When you approach marketing using the Three A's, you can be assured nobody will do what you do exactly like you do, because there is nobody exactly like you. The beauty of being yourself is you *are* your brand.

THE THREE A'S AND TRUST

It's curious that trust is a predictor of a positive therapeutic alliance, and therapeutic alliance is an indicator of positive therapeutic progress. Trust is also the final phase of the marketing funnel before a potential client makes a decision to hire you. Potential clients experience an improvement between making the telephone call to schedule their session and the actual first session. By the time your potential client arrives in the therapy room and meets you for the first time, they are often feeling better, more empowered. I believe the client gets to know you long before they contact you. The big question for you is, *How do I begin to form a therapeutic alliance based on trust before my client meets me?*

Brand predictability. That is the answer. Brand predictability, which translates to you being yourself wherever people find your name. Building trust is accomplished with consistent, reliable communication. First, let them know you are interested in what troubles them—just as in a therapy session (except the client is not in the room with you). Second, communicate you have an awareness of how difficult it is to be in pain and how difficult it is to suffer. In other words, you validate the difficulty they are having with depression, anxiety, anger, or feeling stuck. After all, you're human too. You are not immune to the same experiences. Third, communicate you know something about a possible solution. You have specialized training and you possess some expertise about their problem, and your potential client wants to know you can help. This is where it is essential you know your own perspective of how you make sense of the world.

In graduate school I remember professors asking the students, "What is your worldview?" I had no idea. Do you? How do you make sense of the world, and can you tell someone how you do so?

A worldview is your philosophy or set of beliefs, based on how you understand reality. It is what you believe to be true. There are many worldviews, and each holds within it a set of basic concepts and assumptions about the world and the universe in which we live. Knowing your worldview as a therapist informs your treatment choices. It is significant in the business of your private practice because it is part of your professional identity. You want to be able to clearly and ethically communicate your identity. Stephen Pepper, an American philosopher and author of *World Hypotheses*, concluded after much study that science and how we understand the world can be boiled down into four categories of explanation:[33]

- Formism: The root metaphor is similarity in form. This is a way of understanding the world through categorizing things by characteristics in form or similar traits. An example is, if the object has feathers and lays eggs, it belongs to the bird category. The *DSM, Diagnostic and Statistical Manual*, and the *ICD, International Classification of Disease*, belong to formism as both are organized through classification or categories of symptoms with distinct traits for disorders

- Mechanism: The root metaphor is like a machine. This is the Western medical model of "fix the broken part and it will fix the whole." This would be like cognitive behavioral therapy. Fix the "bad" thoughts and the whole being will be fixed.

- Contextualism: The root metaphor is history as a process. The function of behavior can only be understood in context. The premise is a behavior is understandable when viewed from the historical learning history of the organism. Behavior can only be understood through the lens of an individual's life history.

- Organicism: The root metaphor is developmental as in a living organism with stages of maturation and integration in nature. Babies crawl before they walk.

How you make sense of the world is your worldview. Knowing your worldview allows you to communicate from a consistent place with your language of how you see problems and solutions. This in turn allows you to connect to your potential client in a predictable manner, which develops trust and brand identity. One worldview is not better than another worldview. Each serves a purpose and is useful.

Before we conclude Section Three: Positioning Your Passion, a final thought: Is marketing advertising? No. Although the words are often used interchangeably, advertising is a slice of the pie called marketing. Advertising is about spreading the word, and marketing is about promoting values. Advertising is always marketing, but marketing is a larger process of promoting value through research, delivery, public relations, and more. It is my experience people's opinion about advertising is that it is all about selling with evil and unethical strategies. Then people make the jump that marketing is the same. Simply not true. If you find yourself uncomfortable and unable to promote your private practice, you need to take a close look at your belief in the value of what you offer.

SUMMARY

The buying cycle is part of the marketing funnel, and attunement, alignment, and alliance are behavioral best practices for both therapy success and marketing success. As we look to the next section, you are well on your way to being able to apply your transferable skills into practical business knowledge with the same insight you have as a healer and to create actionable plans that feel authentic and ethical.

Practical Knowledge and

Business Insight

In this section, we dive into your practical knowledge about business and expand on it. Provided in this section are exercises to help liberate you from the inner critic of your problem-solving mind. A short warning about insight: the insight trap is *inaction*. We can know and have insight and still do nothing. Insight is helpful knowledge when coupled with action. We can understand our thoughts, motivations, and insecurities (insight), and then not engage in practical or effective behaviors. Doubt will creep in because it is part of the entrepreneur's journey, and acceptance is the way to let doubt be part of your journey but not run the show.

You might be asking yourself, *What does practical knowledge have to do with business insight?* Let's talk about one of your clients, any one of them.

Clients often come into therapy with a lot of insight about what is happening in their life and why it is happening. They can explain their family of origin wounds. They have good reasons for why they do what they do. Yet, they have not been able to bring about the change they want to see happen in their life even though they possess a lot of insight. Maybe your client wants to move up in their job or get out of a bad relationship. Perhaps they experienced a trauma that is impacting the way they function in the world. Let's unpack this situation.

I'll start with *insight,* which, according to Merriam-Webster, is the ability to see into a situation or person with understanding. Clients understand their situation but lack the practical knowledge to bring about change. *Practical* describes the actual doing of something; *knowledge* pertains to the fact or condition of knowing something. *Practical knowledge* is both theoretical and acquired experience. Business insight joined together with practical knowledge and a plan of action is the pathway to effective decision making and effective behavior.

Back to your client. What's the problem? Action is needed. ACT says the mind is a great problem-solver that actually keeps us stuck in a problem-solving loop. The loop is insight and practical knowledge without action. Sometimes we need to step away from *solving* into *doing*. Sound easy? It is challenging. Insight does not cause behavior change. Making a commitment to take action does. Your client has insight and needs the piece of being able to commit to practical and intentional steps to reach desired outcomes. It takes boots on the ground. I don't say this lightly: the endeavor of being an entrepreneur in a private practice business is being willing to take action even when your mind tells you otherwise. One idea I propose to new entrepreneurs is that it takes the power of "AND" to get going. You can have thoughts, moods, bodily sensations, AND still take action.

Some juicy questions for you to ponder: *Where do you see yourself and what do you want to be doing one year from today? How about five years from today?* Let's stretch the imagination and say ten years from today. How old will you be? Time marches on. You will be wiser and will have greater practical knowledge and insight about what works and doesn't in life and in business. To begin building your practical knowledge for the future, we will start with the marketplace.

CHAPTER

13

The Marketplace — Size Matters

The title of this chapter may sound a bit provocative. Let me stimulate your curiosity about the size of the marketplace in the mental health and wellness industry. The size is wide, and it penetrates all walks of life across a broad socioeconomic stratosphere. In other words, the industry pierces every aspect of our culture. Because of the size of the marketplace you have options for how you choose to develop your business model.

Now that I have your attention, I am going to talk about a few business terms that are relevant to the success of your private practice. However, they aren't very sexy terms. I am going to talk about **absolute market share**, **relative market share**, and **target market** along with **market segmentation**. "Width" and "depth," which are sexy-sounding terms, refer to how you use the marketplace for attracting clients.

Are your eyes glazed over? Stay with me. I'll make this as quick and painless as possible. You do not need to have a comprehensive understanding or deep knowledge of the concepts of absolute and relative market share for you to benefit from being acquainted with them. The importance of the concepts is in allowing you to gain a perspective on a few economic principles. They have greater implications for group practices and nonprofits, though a solo entrepreneur is still wise to have an informed view of the competitive market.

MONEY SHAME

Straight facts about the marketplace are rarely enough to make informed decisions about business matters, as there are psychological factors at play too. Money shame and money guilt creep into conversations when therapists and coaches discuss fees, profits, and business growth. More than once I have heard other professionals talking about the ethics of being on insurance panels and the responsibility of offering low fees so everybody can get help.

A while back, a colleague brought up the concept of money shame. We'll call her Jamie. It is her experience that money shame is a very real problem for counselors and therapists in private practice; it is because of money shame that many practices fail. We hide money shame with language couched in caring and concern for our clients, so we don't ask for fees, and then we give our services away for almost free. But frequently our money shame touches on some very deep issues around our own worthiness and fear. Money shame slithers in when we turn our eyes toward profit, hoping to avoid the self-recrimination of wanting to make money while helping people. However, this issue touches on anxiety and guilt around the "sins" of greed. Hence, we avoid the topic of money and profitability.

We can learn to accept ourselves as we truly are by being willing to look in the mirror as we stand exposed in our desire for success and sustainability. Profit is the lifeblood of all businesses, including private practice.

Let's turn our attention to the size of the overall mental health marketplace, so you can begin to see where your private practice business will prosper.

THE MARKETPLACE

In 2018 almost one out of every five adults in the United States had some form of mental illness in the preceding year.[34] More than 7 percent of all adults suffered a major case of depression within the same period.[35] The federal Substance Abuse and Mental Health Services Administration (SAMHSA) estimates that fully 23.9 million Americans over the age of twelve were addicted to or abused drugs or alcohol in the year they were surveyed. Diseases such as autism spectrum disorder affect one in sixty-eight children. Clinically significant eating disorders affect twenty million women and ten million men in the United States. One in three seniors dies with Alzheimer's or another dementia. NAMI estimates that 9 percent of the U.S. population suffers from personality disorders including clinically significant depression, schizophrenia, bipolar disorder, and others.[36] One thing can definitely be concluded from these statistics: there are more than enough people in the population who are possible candidates for mental health services.

These statistics define the **marketplace**.

Absolute and relative market share are two terms pointing to the fact there are different ways to measure success. The **absolute market share** defines the percentage of dollars a business makes in comparison to another business. You can say your neighbor has a bigger or smaller bite of the *dollar bills* available. The **relative market share** is the percentage of sales a company attracts in the marketplace. Perhaps your neighbor has a bigger or smaller bite of the *total number of customers.* If I had a greater number of dollar sales for the same number of clients, it means I have a greater *absolute* market share. If I have more clients, I have a greater *relative* market share.

You can have a lot of clients compared to the therapist down the street, which might make you seem more successful (relative market share). For example, a colleague might say, "I have 25 clients"—and you have fewer than that. Or you might be involved in a conversation about money with the colleague across the table, who says, "I make $200 per session and made $150,000 last year" (absolute market share). Your mind goes, *WOW! He is really kicking ass.* Then you compare your success with their numbers.

Don't let your comparative polarized mind run the show. Absolute and relative market share are data that influence your strategy on pricing, marketing, and business growth. This information is to help you in your business, not make you feel less (or better) than.

Now we can talk about some really sexy topics about size, including width and depth. I know you're excited to move on to the next topics.

WIDTH AND DEPTH

Wide and flat or narrow and deep are different ways to determine your approach to boosting your business. Remember those numbers gathered by NAMI and SAMHSA. The marketplace is big enough for a diverse set of mental health and wellness services to be offered by agencies, nonprofits, hospitals, group practices, and you, the solo entrepreneur. Hear me: You are free to structure your private practice business any way you want when it comes to setting your fees, hours of operation, who you work with, and where you offer services. Don't let someone shame you or guilt you into offering your services (your calling) for less. You have a gift. Treasure it.

Wide and flat strategies are intended to appeal to a large number of potential clients. Quite often, the fee structure is low. This approach might be a useful strategy for professionals who want to build up a client base quickly. It might also be a beneficial strategy for someone who recently graduated from school and is working to accumulate hours and experience toward licensure. That being said, I strongly do not recommend this as a long-term, sustainable strategy. It's a sure formula for burnout. Burnout from too many sessions is a path to business failure, in addition to personal and financial stress. If you choose wide and flat, develop a plan to leverage your client base for business and financial growth, such as a schedule of increased fees or as a referral foundation.

Narrow and deep is defined by a specific **target market**, or group of potential clients fitting into a specific category. Let's take the category of trauma, which is narrow within the marketplace. Based on the NAMI and SAMHSA numbers, the likelihood of running out of potential clients is pretty slim. Therefore, the category of trauma is considered deep. You got it. Narrow and deep. A clearly defined population with plenty of potential clients.

Addiction is also narrow and deep. There are a lot of people suffering with addiction-type struggles. In these examples, both trauma and addiction are narrow target markets. However, they are both still pretty broad. How do you stand out as the preferred service provider to someone who is struggling with trauma- or addiction-related issues? The answer is (drumroll) you differentiate yourself (your business) within your target market. The business term for differentiating yourself in your target market is called **market segmentation**. Pretty sexy, huh?

A closer look will help you understand the purpose of segmentation. First, bear in mind that people who are suffering from trauma-related conditions can be further defined. To name a few segments within the target market of trauma: domestic violence, sexual assault, war, childhood abuse, natural disaster, terrorism, and mass shooting. The same type of segmentation can be done for addictions: porn, food, drugs, alcohol, internet, and the list goes on. Also, you can focus on stages or types of recovery, such as nutrition, habit reversal, relapse prevention, or sobriety coaching. You can even differentiate yourself with a particular modality for a target market. This could be EMDR, DBT, CBT, psychodynamic, play therapy, or sand tray. Coaches might use a SMART method or a GROWTH model. Obviously, I use ACT as my foundation for counseling and coaching clients. ACT is what differentiates me in the marketplace; plus, I live it and feel passionate about bringing it to people I serve.

You can work with segments that are an ideal fit for you. Although I am using business terms and marketing concepts, we are talking about people you want to work with, so keep in mind all the exploratory work you have already completed in this book. Just as there is nomenclature or jargon in the therapy world (called "psychobabble" by some), it's also in the business world…maybe it should be called "bizbabble." However, economics is still the study of human behavior. Therapy and business are human-to-human endeavors.

By now you probably have a few clear ideas beginning to emerge about who and how you want to work. The clarity you are gaining is beneficial for you and your potential client. It helps you discover your market segment, which includes your niche. Your niche and market segment are embedded in your target market. When you put together target market, market segmentation, and niche you will know your sweet spot for reaching your ideal client. This is good for you and good for them. You will be able to attract the kinds of clients who feed your soul and financially sustain you.

YOUR TARGET MARKET AND YOUR FEES

Wide and flat:	**Narrow and deep:**
Generally, fees are lower	*Generally, fees are higher*

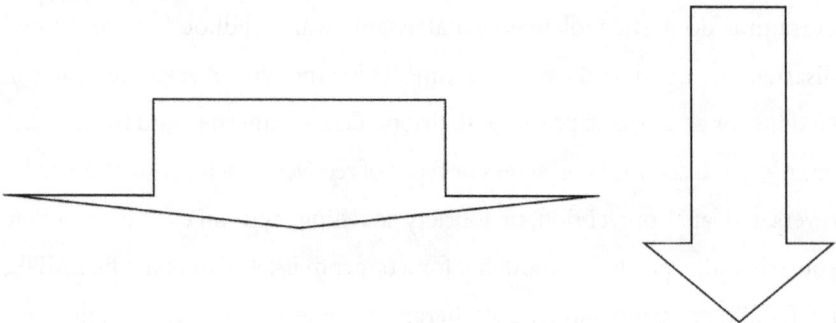

Figure 6: Market Penetration

The wide and flat strategy is used to appeal to the masses by offering low fees—which can be considered a relative market approach as it is aimed at claiming a higher numbers of clients relative to the total number of clients available in your area. This approach attracts a diverse set of people searching for affordable services. It does not mean the only people you will attract will be of a lower socioeconomic status.

Research on perceived pain of paying for products and services has produced a Tightwad-Spendthrift scale. A wide and flat approach most likely will appeal to people with certain personality characteristics, such as being overly frugal or anxious about spending money; they may even be cheap or leaning toward hoarding. I'll just say the frugal consumer tends toward decisions based on the pain of paying and the pleasure of saving. The cool thing about a wide and flat approach is you will attract all kinds of people into your practice. If you are still exploring who you want to work with or what kinds of issues you like to work with, this is an excellent strategy. I used wide and flat in launching my own private practice. It gave me a chance to test my premise in connection to my passions. In the process, I fine-tuned my niche and then moved toward identifying a target market and subsequently identified a segment within the target market.

The opposite of perceived pain of payment is the perceived value of services and willingness to pay. The big takeaway is for you to be able to clearly define your target market in a manner that is narrow but not too narrow and define it so it is deep enough for you to have the opportunity to grow.

PRICING ELASTICITY AND DEMAND

Closely connected to understanding marketplace concepts is pricing knowledge. How will you know the correct price for your services?

Although you may see your calling as sacred, the economics of your service may indicate otherwise. Your services are still subject to the rules of supply and demand. Let me use an illustration taken from Brian Dear, cofounder and CEO of iCouch, Inc.:[37]

> Neurosurgeons provide a service, plumbers provide a service, birthday clowns provide a service. [You] might notice the list is in order of relative importance. If you have a brain tumor, you'd be willing to pay almost anything for the [right] neurosurgeon. [How about the right birthday clown? Would you pay almost anything? Of course not. Would you even hire a birthday clown?] If it's cheap enough, you might consider it, but you're certainly not going to mortgage your house to pay for one. ...
>
> In economic terms, the demand for a neurosurgeon is relatively *inelastic*, while the demand for a clown is very *elastic*.

In other words, the demand for clown services goes up or down, while demand for neurosurgeons remains fairly constant. Hence, demand for a clown is extremely price-sensitive. **Elasticity** is the measure of the price sensitivity of a product or service.

It turns out mental health therapy is more elastic than plumbing services. "If your toilet explodes," Dear points out, "you're definitely calling a plumber; in fact, you're calling him (or her) that instant. If you're having a panic attack, you're rarely going to race to the therapist's office." How we use the finite amount of money we have is based on how important we consider some goods or services to be relative to others.

The formula for pricing elasticity basically states that when the price goes up, the demand goes down. I'll say it again—consumers are price-sensitive to therapy. To translate the Price Elasticity of Demand (PED) formula into everyday language that is useful, let's say you have 15 sessions per week at $85 per session, and you decide to lower your rate by $15 so you end up charging $70 per session. Using the formula, you will have increased demand to 56 sessions per week. Conversely, if you raise your fee to $100, demand will lower to about 13 sessions per week based on the formula.[38]

How about if we play with the numbers a little longer and see how it affects your profits? Really, it's OK to want to make enough money to pay your bills and have some left over for fun and your future. Dear extends the example: figure your business budget is about $3,000 per month with fixed expenses of rent, phone, marketing, professional organizations, continuing education, and insurance. Using the rate of $85 and 100 sessions per month means your revenue will be $8,500 per month and $5,500 after expenses, or $66,000 per year profit.

If you raise your fee to $100 per session, based on the formula, you will have 90 sessions per month. However, your revenue will increase to $9,000. Hence, you have given yourself a raise of $500 per month or $6,000 per year. What would happen if you set your fee at $150 per session? Again, based on the formula, Dear calculates you would be conducting 72 sessions per month with revenue of $10,800 per month. As you raise your fees, the demand for your services decreases but your revenue goes up until you reach a ceiling (supply and demand equilibrium quotient). What will be your best strategy as you grow your business and as your client case load changes? Remember self-care is part of appropriate and responsible therapeutic work—burnout does not have to be part of the job.

A word of caution: setting low fees will not guarantee you clients. You still need to have a marketing plan. In addition to understanding pricing elasticity, it is useful to understand another formula on the distribution of your clients and the services you offer, called the Pareto Principle.

PARETO PRINCIPLE: THE 80/20 RULE

The Pareto Principle is best known as the 80/20 rule, which states that roughly 80 percent of results come from 20 percent of effort.[39] In 1941, management consultant, Joseph M. Juran stumbled across a paper written by Italian economist Vilfredo Pareto in 1896, based on an observation of the distribution of wealth. Approximately 80 percent of the land was owned by 20 percent of the population. Pareto also observed 20 percent of the peapods in his garden produced 80 percent of the peas.

The Pareto Principle is not a law of nature but an observation of the distribution of results. The 80/20 rule is a rule of thumb. When applied to the business world, the Pareto Principle suggests 80 percent of your revenue comes from 20 percent of your clients. This is another reason to get clear about your niche within your target market. When you have clarity about whom you want to serve, you can maximize your efforts to connect with the 20 percent who are the best match. Chances are, based on the Pareto Principle, you will still attract people outside your niche.

PARETO AND PRODUCTIVITY

The Pareto Principle can be applied to productivity as well. The 96-minute rule is a guideline for increasing productivity and, yes, it is based on the Pareto Principle.[40] The guideline suggests that in an average eight-hour workday, 20 percent of your time (96 minutes) should be dedicated to your most important work. In other words, 96 minutes will produce 80 percent of your results. Since you have two major roles, one being a therapist and the other being a business owner, you can spend 96 minutes of the first part of your workday on the business. The optimal productivity derived from the 96-minute rule is to work without multitasking, distractions, or interruptions. How does this sound to you? Are you willing to dedicate 96 minutes per day for business and then put on your therapist's hat? Of course, some of you might want to pick a different time of day to dedicate 96 minutes to the tasks of running a business. That's OK as long as you make enough alone time to give your full attention to your project.

To further understand the importance of dedicated time, let's take a look at a study conducted by Basex, Inc., a research firm.[41] Basex found workers are distracted on average 2.1 hours per day or about 28 percent of the workday, and this statistic includes recovery time. Recovery time is how long it takes to return to the same level of productivity before the distraction. What are the implications of this study for your business? Distractions can burgeon out of control, robbing you of precious time and energy.

You need to know what you want to devote your attention to during your workday, so it's a good idea to have a plan. Don't do as I did. I allowed social media to interrupt me in the beginning (I sometimes still do), and my project took a back seat as I struggled to get back on task. This is when Eye on the Prize comes in handy. Also, here we come back to the importance of having a vision statement and a mission statement, and, hopefully, a basic business plan.

Keep Your Eye on the Prize Exercise

Are you willing to engage in another experiential exercise? You might have heard the phrase, "Keep your eye on the prize." With your full participation in this exercise, you will experience what it means to walk your talk. Do this exercise and you will have access to a procedural memory experience in your behavioral data bank. The benefit of procedural memory will be an increase in your ability to recall how to move toward your prize. Read through the exercise, then come back and complete it. I promise this one will pay off. Eye on the Prize takes about 15 to 30 minutes.

Materials

- One piece of typing paper (or larger if you have it)

- 1 marker

- 20 pieces of paper about 3x5 inches. (index cards work great if you have them)

- 1 pencil or pen for notes

Instructions

On the typing paper using the marker, write in bold letters your desired dream goal, such as: Open a Private Practice. Once you have written your dream goal, draw some cool pictures on it too. Tape the completed sign on the wall or a door. This is your prize. It is special to you.

With the pen or pencil, and the twenty pieces of 3x5 papers in hand, step back from your prize as far back as you can while still being able to clearly see it, ideally about ten to fifteen feet. Question: *What are the steps you need to take to accomplish your dream goal?* Keep looking at the prize. *What's the next step after you finish reading this book?* Write the step on a piece of paper and set it on the floor about six inches from the tip of the toes of your right foot. Again notice what shows up on the inside. What is your mind telling you? Any thoughts about fear or doubt like, *I don't know enough yet, so I better read another book*? Write the thought on a piece of paper and set it on the floor about six inches out from the tip of your toes of your left foot. Look up; keep your eye on the prize. Your right foot is staying on the path of moving toward your prize. Your left foot represents a detour off the path to your dream goal.

Next take nine pieces of paper and write on each piece one step you are going to take toward your prized goal. Then lay them out as a path toward the prize on the floor by your right foot. Have fun.

Take the remaining nine pieces of paper and write on each one a detour that might show up. You know yourself well enough to know your detours. Lay the detours on the floor in front of your left foot, next to the right-foot path.

Learning takes place as you move between both paths. With your eye on the prize, walk both the directed path and the detour back and forth, right step, left step, side to side. Showing yourself it's possible to get detoured and get back on the path. Practice noticing when you are on the path. Practice noticing when you are detoured. Notice all three: the path, the detour, and the prize. Once in a while, glance down and see what is written on the pieces of paper. The motion of walking will keep you moving forward even when you find yourself detoured. Getting off track on a detour still provides you with information for the next step or next challenge. Keep moving forward as you go from left to right while keep your eye on the prize.

Final suggestion: Gather all the pieces of paper including your prize, which can be written on a piece of pocket-sized paper, and carry them around for a week in your pocket or purse. Take a peek are least once a day. If the pieces of paper get out of order notice what you think and feel. I wonder what you'll notice when the prize shows up as you peek. Noticing is a skill to increase awareness.

You might be tempted to believe your mind when it tells you, "I don't need to do Eye on the Prize. I read it. That's good enough." Don't be silly. You can't learn to swim by reading a book. Entrepreneurship is outside your comfy zone. By doing the Eye on the Prize exercise you learn how to navigate detour temptation and walk your talk. You will learn what willingness feels like. You will gain working knowledge. The more you are willing to do this for yourself, the more you gain as a skill to share and teach others. The cool thing about experiential exercises is the physical engagement with your whole being—your body learns to *do*.

If you find yourself unable to stay focused on your business priorities, there are plenty of apps to choose from to help you focus. I like RescueTime. The app helped me cut down on social media distractions to one hour a day. I downloaded it on my desktop, but you can download an app to your tablet, pad, or phone. It nudges me in the direction of awareness.

PARETO AND THE SERVICES YOU PROVIDE

Applying the 80/20 rule to the types of services you provide to your clients can be insightful. Understanding these services through the lens of the 80/20 rule will allow you to shape and grow your private practice business in a meaningful direction. Are you ready to generate ideas about services that might appeal to your target market? Yes. Let's get generating ideas to help you find clarity in defining a wide and flat or a narrow and deep market. Let's take a look at mind mapping to generate ideas. Mind Mapping refers to a process called whole brain thinking and/or radiant thinking. Whatever you call it: mind mapping, radiant thinking, whole brain…the processes are all the same.

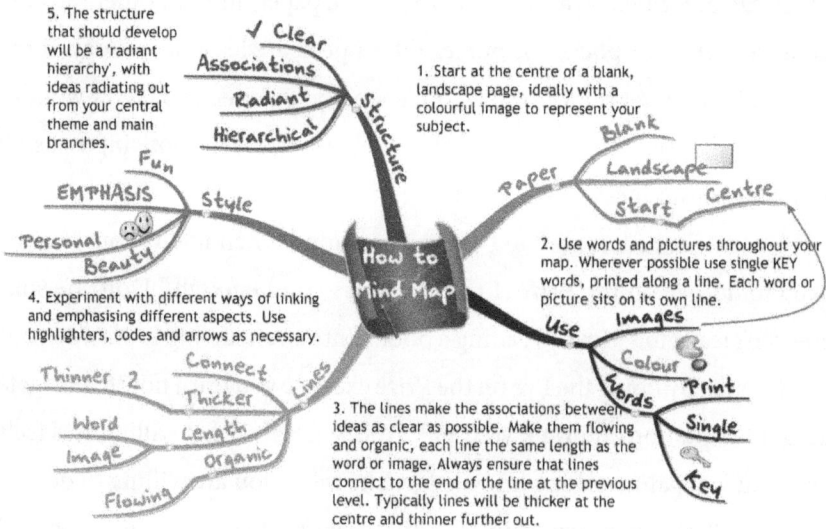

5. The structure that should develop will be a 'radiant hierarchy', with ideas radiating out from your central theme and main branches.

1. Start at the centre of a blank, landscape page, ideally with a colourful image to represent your subject.

2. Use words and pictures throughout your map. Wherever possible use single KEY words, printed along a line. Each word or picture sits on its own line.

4. Experiment with different ways of linking and emphasising different aspects. Use highlighters, codes and arrows as necessary.

3. The lines make the associations between ideas as clear as possible. Make them flowing and organic, each line the same length as the word or image. Always ensure that lines connect to the end of the line at the previous level. Typically lines will be thicker at the centre and thinner further out.

Figure 7: How to Mind Map

Mind Maps Exercise

A mind map is a wonderful process sure to delight your creative side and unite it with your logical side. Completing a mind map will allow you to create a whole picture of your target market, then hone in on what appeals to you. It also helps define where the 80/20 rule might come into play. Even if you are not sure about your target market, you will discover many available avenues to fulfillment through the process. Mind mapping is a mnemonic tool with a high utility for a variety of tasks, including time management, study skills, presentation formats, and more.

Let's go back to the earlier example of working with trauma survivors or working with addictions. Ask yourself, *What or whom do you want to work with?* Once you answer the question, place the answer in the center of the page. Ask yourself probing questions as if you are a detective looking for clues to who your ideal client is and when, where, what, and how you connect with them. *What is the value you provide to your ideal client? How will they benefit from seeing you? All the while record your answers in one or two words on your mind map. When do you want to work (time of day and days of the week)?* Ask yourself questions about your client: *What stage of life are they in as far as age or stage of recovery? Where are they in their life journey that appeals to you? Do you want to provide group therapy or psycho-educational therapy for groups? How about a support group? Will you offer presentations to your target audience?*

Not sure if a mind map will be useful? Try it as an experiment with a sense of curiosity.

Mind Map Instructions

- Start with a central image. It can be a word or a picture

- Use three or more colors when making the mind map

- Keep your paper placed horizontally in front of you

- Draw images throughout as clearly as possible

- Use variations of size of printing, lines, and images

- Use branching or fishbone connections

- Use hierarchy or numerical order when called for

- Connect lines to other lines for repeating themes

- Include feelings or sensory experiences

- Let your style and imagination flow

- Date the back of your mind map

I like to share my mind map with someone who will interview me about the details on it. Then I display my treasured mind map in a place where I see it on a daily basis. Once finished you have whole concepts about your business and clients to flesh out your business plan. Who will interview you about your mind map?

SUMMARY

Knowledge of the economic landscape of the marketplace, with a basic understanding of target market, market segment, and niche, gives you the vision to wisely develop a purposeful strategy for attracting clients. Pricing and profits are not as straightforward as they appear on the surface. It's possible you can work less and make more. There is an art to the mission of entrepreneurship as a vision for your future.

Knowing in advance what your goals are will help you decide if you want a wide and flat strategy or a narrow and deep strategy. I know it's sexy to understand how size matters when it comes to the ideas of narrow and deep as strategies. Each of these concepts has its pros and cons. Knowledge is a protective shield from being caught up in the winds of evaluative comparison to others—something our minds are good at. There is no absolute right strategy that guarantees profitability. Nor is there an ideal fee you should charge for your services. The point is to be purposeful in setting out what you aim to accomplish. Being purposeful is the best guarantee of success. Now that we have looked at size matters, we can tackle who else serves your client beyond the services you offer.

CHAPTER

14

Who Serves Your Clients (and Beyond)

The well-being of the country and the community is dependent on a network of healthcare providers who offer services to the population in the form of treatment, prevention, and diagnosis of illness, injury, and disease. Therapists are part of the healthcare network. Know your network so you can develop strategic relationships to grow your private practice and provide a standard of care in alignment with your values and the clients' needs. Part of that strategy is cross-pollination. It is a concept taken from nature and applied to business environments. Cross-pollination can take place within a business or among businesses. The rationale behind cross-pollination is to bring people together from diverse backgrounds to allow the flow of knowledge and skills to build a stronger entity within the company and within the community. We'll dive deeper into cross-pollination in the chapter. Who is in your community?

The National Center for Complementary and Integrative Health breaks down the different types of providers into categories of professionals who offer services to the same clients you serve.[42]

10 Most Common Complementary Health Approaches Among Adults—2012

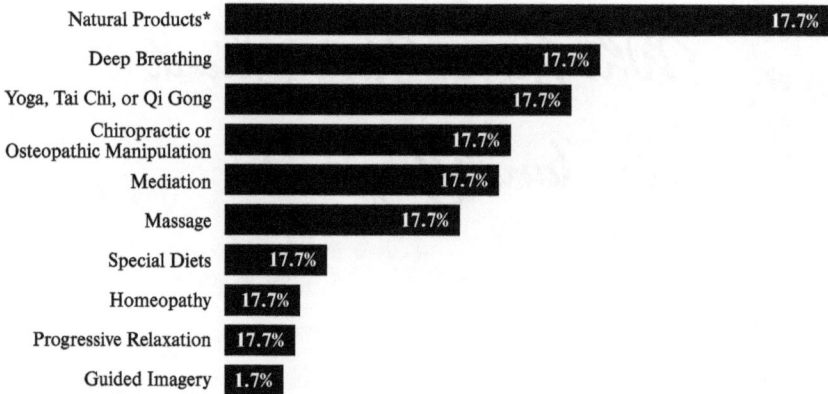

Approach	Percentage
Natural Products*	17.7%
Deep Breathing	17.7%
Yoga, Tai Chi, or Qi Gong	17.7%
Chiropractic or Osteopathic Manipulation	17.7%
Mediation	17.7%
Massage	17.7%
Special Diets	17.7%
Homeopathy	17.7%
Progressive Relaxation	17.7%
Guided Imagery	1.7%

Figure 8: 10 Most Common Complementary Health Approaches, courtesy of the National Center for Complementary and Integrative Health.

Many people go outside traditional Western care for their healthcare. About 30 percent of adults and 12 percent of children use approaches considered as complementary or alternative. Complementary is care used in conjunction with traditional medical care; alternative methods are used as a stand-alone approach to healthcare. Integrative care focuses on a more holistic approach, emphasizing care of the whole person, including mental, emotional, spiritual, social, functional, and community aspects. The aim is to provide well-coordinated care with an emphasis on being client focused rather than organ focused; this care may include a variety of providers or institutions. Also, eye doctors, dentists, audiologists, and midwives are considered allied healthcare professionals.[43] You might be asking yourself how to begin participation in the multifaceted allied healthcare community. One tool for connecting I wish I would have known about from the beginning is cross-pollination.

CROSS-POLLINATION

The birds do it. The bees do it. And you can do it. In the plant and animal world, cross-pollination produces organisms that are stronger, more disease resistant and genetically diverse, with healthier offspring, thereby, quickening evolution. Why is this important? Similar benefits occur in the business world. Cross-pollination allows you to have a stronger and more diverse network, thereby supporting your chances of sustained success.

Cross-pollination supports continuity of care. *Entrepreneur* magazine reports on studies indicating that businesses grow faster, increase productivity, and have higher revenue when they participate in forming alliances with other businesses.[44] Additionally, cross-pollination within an organization (across different departments) increases innovation. Pretty cool stuff if you ask me. It works the same for you and your private practice. Cross-pollination strengthens your business through diversity of ideas and practices. You place your private practice business in a position that promotes a wider perspective of your client and how your services support your client. Additionally, you gain a bigger picture of how your services fit into the larger healthcare community.

I refer to these other providers who serve your clients as an **auxiliary tribe**. You can learn from your auxiliary tribe by keeping an open mind and listening. Approach the relationship with members of your auxiliary tribe with the same set of values you use in serving your clients. Keep in mind to complement, and not cannibalize, the members of your auxiliary tribe.

Look back, as you are now in a position to conclude why it is important to have a clear idea of your target market, your market segment, and your niche—so you can identify who is in your auxiliary tribe. Who serves your clients? Think about the demographic and psychographic description of the population you serve.

Do you like brainstorming? Yes, you say. Fantastic! Together, let's brainstorm and come up with ideas for cross-pollination with an auxiliary tribe by poring over who, when, where, and how to cross-pollinate with. Why we cross-pollinate is to build a referral stream and support continuity of care.

AUXILIARY TRIBE

Meet a hypothetical client, Sally. She is a thirty-four-year-old Hispanic female. Sally is married with two children, a ten-year-old boy and a seven-year-old daughter. Her children attend a private Catholic school. Sally is bilingual and works as an administrative assistant at a construction company. She has some college credit and wants to return to school. Sally is a survivor of childhood sexual abuse. She is seeking therapy because of stress and anxiety. She claims her stress and anxiety are a problem, and she fears it is interfering with her marriage. Additionally, she has chronic pain in her lower back from an injury in her teens, and this seems to hold her back from activities. Her primary care physician (PCP) prescribed Prozac for anxiety. Deep in Sally's heart, she wants to not have to depend on medication. Her strength is her determination and resolve to live a fulfilling life. Her mantra is, "It's a big world," which to Sally means she wants to fully experience life and the world.

Now that you have met Sally, you can use this information to help serve her and build connections. Follow along as we explore how to build an auxiliary tribe. Your purpose in making contact with service providers is to build relationships. You can reach out before you have a client. It's never too early to grow connections. Create a list of a few providers in your neighborhood.

Start on the Auxiliary Tribe contact list with the Hansel and Gretel Contact Form you can download from my website. Remember not to cannibalize; be sure ask who their ideal client is, so you can refer to them in turn. Also, be mindful about HIPAA regulations and respect for privacy.

Who and How

I will stay with Sally for the purpose of illustration, but you can extrapolate from your particular choices. Think in terms of what you can do now to start cross-pollinating and growing your auxiliary tribe. It's never too soon. Take a moment to bring to mind your niche and/or your ideal client. Who is your Sally? How and with whom might she be served beyond the therapy hour she spends with you?

If Sally is my client, I begin with contacting the Rape, Abuse & Incest National Network (RAINN). There's a chapter in almost every state. You can do this before you have a client like Sally. I will contact a local chapter and ask them for a tour and an interview. When I have a chance, I meet with an outreach personnel at RAINN and pick up a handful of brochures for Sally or other future clients in my niche.

Almost every business, agency, or office has a liaison who acts as the information person or as outreach for the community. When I meet with that liaison, I offer my business card or any other marketing collateral. Even if you are a student, get some business cards printed. That's right—you can have business cards printed up before you open a private practice; your name and number with your tagline are sufficient for a start. Be sure to leave your contact information with the person you speak to. The new wave for business cards is digital. There are several apps you can use: SnapDat, CamCard, Haystack, and EVault offer free versions.

Back to Sally. She is a sexual abuse survivor, so I look further for support services for future information. The objective is to create contacts with people I can grow professional relationships with.

Start making a list of organizations, agencies, and people who might offer auxiliary services. For example, look for a local agency of the National Organization for Victim Assistance (NOVA). Most county courts also have victim advocates and agencies. Hospitals are a great place to start building relationships with emergency room nurses and social workers.

When Sally comes in for her first appointment to complete paperwork, I ask her to sign a release of information (ROI) so I can contact her PCP, either with a phone call or letter. A letter is preferable, as it serves a dual purpose of coordination of care and cross-pollination. I include a copy of the ROI in the letter to the PCP or fax it in advance. Of course, if she prefers not to sign an ROI, that is OK. Consent is of the utmost importance. If Sally does not want me to contact her PCP, I will ask her if there is another person she would like me to talk with as a way to coordinate her care.

During our sessions, I learn Sally sees a massage therapist and a nutritionist for pain management and diet to lose weight. Great! I ask Sally if it is OK that I contact them, and if so, I get an ROI for them too. I reach out to Sally's massage therapist and nutritionist, probably in a less formal way than I do with a PCP. I call and coordinate care of client with Sally's massage therapist and nutritionist. If Sally prefers for me not to mention her I might still call the providers. I will absolutely not mention Sally, because I want to protect her privacy, Since I am connecting in a less formal way (not to talk about Sally) I call to invite the person for coffee or tea. Be careful to protect your client!

Many of these people and organizations are considered complementary allied service providers—they provide services that have an indirect benefit to a client in supporting a sense of well-being. It's the icing on the cake. Relationships with complementary healthcare service providers are cost-effective for your private practice in the long run, once a trusted relationship is established. One referral from your tribe is worth a thousand views from a source such as an online directory.

When meeting providers, one of the last questions I ask is who else they would recommend that I can contact. Remember the etiquette for informational interviews in Chapter 7 and take a token gift, such as gourmet jelly beans, and always be respectful of their time. Also remember the Hansel and Gretel Contact Form and use it with service providers.

Where and When

When you contact potential members of your auxiliary tribe, find out where they want to meet. Some people work out in the field and welcome a chance to meet in an office environment. Others love to get out of the office for a cup of coffee or tea. A few might want to scope out your digs. This might seem obvious, but it never hurts to spell out the process. Do they have a favorite café or park? Would they like to meet via phone or video chat? The bottom line is you want to make it convenient for them. Be flexible. If you are contacting a doctor, you may offer to meet with their staff instead.

One sure way to turn them off is if you make it all about you. Spend a little bit of time learning something about the person or business before meeting them. This is similar to what you did for conducting informational interviews. Don't show up with the expectation they are going to give you something, like client referrals. Don't be a cannibal. Nobody likes a cannibal. You are connecting so you can build a relationship with other professionals who serve your clients. Use the Three A's of attunement, alignment, and alliance.

COMMUNICATION IS KEY

As you grow your tribe, which includes therapists, allied healthcare professionals, and complementary service providers, it is prudent to develop a system to follow the communication trail. The objective is to find your way back through the history to the beginning of your relationship. Again, use the Hansel and Gretel Contact Form.

You can use paper or digital methods. Use what works for you. Include in the system a way to know if you have connected through warm or cold touches. A **warm touch** is personal, involving information about the person beyond the role they are in when doing their job. An example of a warm touch is if you know the person is a fan of a band, a sports team, or has a hobby such as gardening. Talk with them about their personal interests. For example, send an email, "Hi Lynn, I saw your favorite football team won this weekend by a landslide." Or, "Are you going to the Rolling Stones concert?" "I am sending you an article about a new product to use on Orchids to help them bloom. It's called Green Jungle." A **cold touch** is a business touch, such as sending them articles of professional interest. For example, a massage therapist might like to know about recent research on the healing effects of massage for trauma survivors. Doctors might be interested in innovation of equipment and procedures for treatment and diagnosis. In the end you want to provide useful, pertinent information related to their profession. Then you want to sprinkle in a few warm touches in your communication. Be authentic and show genuine interest, nothing fake or phony. Engage in a brief conversation about their interests. If you don't know anything about their interests, be curious. You got this. Curiosity's another therapy skill. You want to create a balance between warm and cold touch.

See how it goes. A professional acquaintance I knew got married in Dallas and they are fans of the Dallas Cowboys football team. They honeymooned in Hawaii. Both pieces of this information lend themselves to a warm touch. I sent a message when I heard the Dallas Cowboys won one of their games. It was quick and short. I asked if they watched the game. As for the honeymoon, would you believe it snowed three feet in Hawaii in December that year? Now that is something to talk about!

You can find plenty of good topics for warm touches. Sincerity is the secret ingredient. Even a simple message such as "Happy Anniversary" is a warm touch. We all like to be remembered.

The Hansel and Gretel system is ideal for the introvert who tends to avoid large networking groups. If you are an extrovert, it works just as well. I keep about ten to twenty active Hansel and Gretel Contacts in my active list in a binder for building relationships. As business contacts come and go I keep all of the active ones toward the front of my binder. I alphabetize for record keeping.

Use your time wisely and nurture the relationships that are good fits. Some of my deepest friendships have grown from this system. As you begin building relationships, remember to record your relationship information or use the Hansel and Gretel Contact Form for contacts. You can download sample cross-pollination letters for allied providers from my website.

If you receive a referral that came from another therapist in your peer group, send a thank you card acknowledging their trust in you. The foundational gesture in cross-pollinating is a place of giving support. Ask, "How can I best support you?" Carry this attitude with you. Listen first to understand their needs. Where else can you travel to find fertile ground to cross-pollinate?

BEYOND ALLIED HEALTHCARE PROVIDERS

Cross-pollination can take place in other fertile environments structured to breed creativity, be supportive, offer problem solving, and hold each other accountable.

Mastermind Groups

The term mastermind came from American author Napoleon Hill, who coined the phrase "Master Mind Alliance" in his 1928 book, *The Law of Success*. In a most straightforward sense, a mastermind group is a group of two to seven people who meet on a regular schedule to support each other in attaining specific goals. You can join a mastermind group or start your own.

Members of a mastermind group can be from diverse backgrounds with similar goals. The advantage of having people from different professions is they will offer a different perspective. Joining a mastermind group with people who are all therapists, on the other hand, can bring together knowledge like a living encyclopedia. Peer consultation groups would fall into the category of a hybrid mastermind group with a specific purpose of increasing knowledge, skills, and accountability. People within the group often refer clients to one another because the members are considered vetted. The important piece to joining or starting a mastermind or peer group is to be sure it is functional and the group facilitator is skilled at creating harmony and safety, so the members feel they can speak openly. Don't know where to start? Try Meetup or Craigslist.

To start your own consultation group, announce it on a social media platform such as Facebook. It is a great opportunity for someone new to practice small group skills and get to know others in the community. Be ready to take responsibility for facilitating the functioning of the group if you start one.

Personal Board of Directors

Sometimes referred to as a "circle of trust," a personal board of directors is composed of a few people you can trust to be honest advisors and guides. This means not your family and friends. Too close. Your board can be small with just two or three people. You want to invite members who, as a group, will provide you with money smarts, be capable of telling the white-hot truth, and be connectors. Include someone from the private practice sector in your field of interest and someone younger who knows what's cool. If possible, recruit people who are motivating and inspiring, yet compassionate and gentle when necessary.

Together, the members offer psychosocial and career support. Sometimes a personal board of directors is called a "personal board of advisors" or a "personal board of mentors," which ensures the group is immune from the formal rules of a corporate board of directors, and you retain the power to have the final say. In other words, keep it casual, even if you decide to hold quarterly meetings with all the members of your board. You don't want it to become a time and energy drain.

Meetings can be held on a platform like Google Hangouts or Zoom. Keep a running list of questions for your meetings. Between meetings, use the members of the board for specific topics within their scope of interest or expertise. Know who you can turn to when you need advice, guidance, or support. It is a good idea to title or define each role as the board is formed. Once you ask a person to join your board, find out how they see their role— mentor, advisor, guide? Write them a letter (snail mail or email) to confirm their position and role. You do not need to pay your board, although you absolutely need to show them appreciation. Most of all, they will want to know they make a difference, so be specific about how they impact your life, your business, and your success. Use your board wisely by listening and getting rid of the *yeah but* language. *Yeah but* is a surefire way to sabotage a well-functioning board. Keep it simple. Pick and choose what works for you.

Mentors

Once upon a time mentoring was popular and a strategic way to learn the ropes to success. Finding and picking a mentor is one of the easiest ways to grow your professional development and to cross-pollinate. You can have more than one mentor, and meetings can be as casual or formal as needed. It is a good idea to pick a mentor who is a few stages ahead of you in professional development and business skills.

It is best to spell out what you bring to the relationship as a mentee. How do you show up? What are you eager to learn? Are you dependable and a good listener? Do you need help with risk-taking, or follow-through? Do you need help setting goals? One of my favorite mentors shared early on in our relationship their wish for me was to exceed their success. I understand now what that meant. They wanted the best for me even if they were left behind. It felt like a good parent relationship.

Coaches

You can hire a coach for just about anything. A good business coach is invaluable. Like good therapists, they are in the position to help you figure it out for yourself. Sure, they can provide answers and offer you guidance, but the real value in a coach comes from the freedom of being in your own creative space. An effective coach helps you tap into your strengths. Plus, you may experience a coaching relationship as being collaborative, like a partnership.

A coach can see your blind spots and shed light on them while being your biggest cheerleader. Most coaches have formal training, but many bring their real-life experience to the relationship. The range of expense to hire a coach can be as low as $50 per hour to as high as $400 per hour. Most coaches offer packages that make them more affordable. A coach does not have to have experience in your specific field, although there are some real advantages to hiring a coach who knows the ins and outs.

Special Mention for Networking

The Small Business Administration (SBA) in your community is worth checking into. The objective of the SBA is to help you plan, build, launch, and grow your business. Under the umbrella of the SBA are the Office of Small Business and Development Centers (OSBDC) and SCORE, which stands for Service Corps of Retired Executives. The Chamber of Commerce is also an option.

As you look into resources, be sure you get enough information before attending a meeting or joining an organization to be sure it is a good fit. Be prepared, as costs of time and money can add up quickly. Most organizations I mention here have fees. One of the largest business referral networking groups, called Business Networking International (BNI), has chapters worldwide in seventy countries and offers multiple locations in major cities. Membership stands at 230,000 people worldwide.

Once you scope out a few networking groups, pick one or two to attend on a regular basis for at least a year. I suggest a year of regular attendance so people can get to know you, like you, trust you, and then refer people to you—and vice versa. Limit yourself to three groups maximum. You don't want to spread yourself too thin. See the References and Additional Resources section for more.

COMFORT ZONE

Most therapists are comfortable networking with other therapists in their peer group. When you contemplate cross-pollinating activities and opportunities, you will need to get outside of your comfort zone. Most of us, when we go outside our comfort zone, will experience thoughts and feelings of insecurity, anxiety, and shyness. Not a problem. I have a few more defusion skills that can come in handy:

- Treat your thoughts like guests entering a hotel. You can be like the doorman: you greet the guests, but you don't follow them to their rooms

- Observe your thoughts as if they are clouds in the sky floating by

- Notice your thoughts like leaves on a stream floating away

- Put your thoughts in or on a car, train, boat, or plane, and watch them go by as you sit as a spectator

- Act as if you were a curious scientist observing thoughts for the very first time

- Where are your thoughts in relation to your body? Top, bottom, front, back, side, outside?

The purpose of these defusion approaches is NOT, I repeat NOT, to get rid of your discomfort. The purpose of developing defusion skills is to expand in your ability to be willing to feel what you feel and still take action on your values. You are building a larger menu in your behavior repertoire.

SUMMARY

Build a community. Build your tribe. Call it what you want. The objective of "Who Serves Your Client, and Beyond?" is to get you thinking about building strategic relationships in the community where your private practice business lives and thrives. There is a community of service providers offering support services to your ideal client. How you connect is something you can customize to your personal preferences. You can write cross-pollination letters, get releases of information, and make phone calls to offer continuity of care. You also can set up consultation calls for coordination of care. Design something that fits you. Your objective is to connect to people you can relate to and have mutuality with as a two-way street. Included in this chapter are other networking opportunity and business support systems beyond allied health care professionals, such as mastermind groups. Be purposeful and strategic, and remember to give back.

CHAPTER

15

Effective Tools and Teams

One theme every entrepreneur wrestles with is time management. Failing to develop effective time management skills leads to stress, decreased productivity, lack of efficiency, burnout, and general lack of focus. Time management boils down to focusing skills—mindfulness and purposeful behavioral choices that serve your values. There is a clear and direct link to your future based on your ability to focus your behavior today.

Your sweet spot is in finding the right balance of hat-wearing. Burnout is greatly reduced with your ability to find a balanced mixture of doing it yourself, delegating to contracted service professionals, and running automated programs. Balancing is a learned skill. It is having boundaries. You know this from helping clients with boundaries.

Time management choices include the people you pick for support services for your private practice business. Who you pick to be in your corner should be part of a strategic plan. Think about building a team for your budding business. It may seem lofty to have a team from the beginning. I get it. You have few or no clients, with little means of revenue to hire a team to support you. I'm here to reassure you that you can build a small team of support personnel with a next-to-nothing, low-cost budget. How? By starting out with a straightforward look at time management, you will discover a menu of options for making effective choices on team building.

One thing for sure: building a support team with the right mix of people, services, and strategies will boost your overall success now and in the long run. Let's start off by reviewing the Magical Bank and time management.

SPENDING TIME

Remember the Magical Bank of winning $86,400 a day in Chapter 10? You have a finite amount of time to spend in any one day. Wisely spending and allotting your time and money on the activities that serve your business and clients is a tricky balancing act.

Meet Heather (not her real name), one of my coaching clients. Heather complains she *always* feels "on" and she *never* has time for herself. I know *always* and *never* are extreme words and fit into a category of catastrophic thinking. Yet, her experience is not uncommon and not to be dismissed. I hear it often. What is interesting is that one of the motivating factors of why people go into business for themselves is so they can be in control of their destinies. Entrepreneurship attracts people with a desire for control of financial success, emotional independence, and freedom of time. The feeling of being "on" all the time defeats the underlying drive and purpose of entrepreneurship. So, what's the fix?

Perception and reality are quite often different. To begin, I assigned Heather a tracking task to increase her awareness of how she is actually spending her time. (An example follows below in Figure 9.) To start, she recorded her day-to-day expenditures of time over a two-week period. Then we took a broad overview of her month-to-month plans for a full calendar year. This is a great way to gain perspective on the flow of activities in your life. This process will eventually help you choose a time management system that is a good fit for your organizational skills and time management skills. The whole process is three steps: tracking, plotting (mapping), and maintaining—how you spend your time (tracking), how you plan to spend your time (mapping/plotting), and reinforcing effective time management (maintaining). Once you see the big picture of how you spend your time, it will be easy to build your team with the right people and tools. Let's get down to the nuts and bolts.

Where and how to start? Start where you are, just as you do with clients. What's going on now? Pretend you are doing an intake on yourself on how you currently manage your time. What does your average day and week look like? You are creating a baseline of your current "spending" system. This is central to measure and understand your natural personal energy cycle. Keep in mind, the purpose of tracking, plotting, and maintaining is so you can make prudent decisions for building a support system with suitable people and useful tools. It's your turn to track and plot. The maintenance piece comes after tracking and plotting.

Track and Plot Your Personal Energy Cycle Exercise

We all have prime-time energy and downtime energy, called circadian rhythms. You might consider yourself a night owl or an early bird or a midday performer. We all experience times when we perform more effectively. You and I have an internal clock. When you are aware of your internal clock and circadian rhythms, you are able to leverage the natural cycle for optimal use of your energy.

Our first step is the creation of a baseline calendar over two weeks. When your baseline calendar is complete, you will use it to develop a schedule for optimal use of your energy and time.

MATERIALS

Paper calendar with 24 hours a day for 7 days of the week for 2 full weeks. You can print a free blank calendar from the internet or from Microsoft Word.

Colored pencils or markers to differentiate categories of activities.

Figure 9: Circadian Rhythm Tracking

Use the colored pencils or markers for shading in the activities you do throughout the day. Using colors to shade in activities allows you to take a quick glance and see the flow of your personal energy. Assign one task per color. For example: blue for sleep time; green for morning routine of showering, breakfast, and getting kids out the door; orange for drive time; yellow for clients. You get the idea. Be sure to include leisure activities like TV, family, and self-care. The purpose is to chart your daily activities by tracking how you are spending your time in *real time*, regardless of what you have scheduled. No judgments. You are measuring your natural energy cycle. In other words, this is NOT your *to-do* list but your *what-you-do* list.

If you want to add one more piece of information to your tracking, make a note of your energy level as being high, medium, or low. This is optional and can be recorded in the shaded areas. When I created my first baseline, I learned my creative prime time was between ten p.m. and two a.m. for writing, and one to six p.m. was my prime high-energy time for seeing clients and completing paperwork. I learned mornings were a downtime, as that was when I had poor focus. Also, you might discover when you procrastinate and what activities are symptoms of procrastination. Hold the judgments! You are in discovery.

Most of us have a natural routine that unfolds throughout the day and throughout the week. You might find your week runs better on a Wednesday through Saturday flow. Be willing to be flexible. It is helpful to know what you already do naturally, rather than imposing rules on how you're supposed to spend your time. After all, it is your time, your life, and you get to choose.

Once you have completed two weeks, you are ready to take a look at how to power up your schedule to match your personal energy cycle. With the baseline of your personal energy cycle highlighting your prime time, you can optimize your schedule to fit your business hours and responsibilities, along with your free time in creating a work/life balance that keeps you focused. You can incorporate this information into your business plan: when you want to see clients during the day and what days of the week you want to see clients. You can decide on billing cycles for accounting purposes. Equally important, although not included in the business plan, is deciding what days you want for yourself and your family, your hobbies and your leisure, your health and your self-care. After all, this is why people become entrepreneurs, so they get to have a say on how they spend their time.

Now that you have an idea for day-to-day planning and accountability, let's look at formatting and plotting a yearly calendar. Effective time management takes time. Hence, allow a few weeks to complete the next project. A time map for plotting your year needs to be done annually. I complete my annual time map in October, so I can hit the ground running when New Year's rolls around. It feels great to start a new year knowing you're ahead of the game. As you map/plot your year, keep in mind your personal energy cycle.

Mapping Your Year Exercise

If you are halfway through the year, start with a plan for now until the end of the year. It's best if you can map and plot for a full twelve months. Like I said, I prefer to complete my annual map and plot the full year in October, as November and December are too busy and are low-energy months.

Step 1. Print out a calendar page for each month of the year. Don't think you can do this by looking at one month at a time on Google Calendar. You can't. Print twelve full months out on twelve pieces of paper. Make sure you print a calendar with holidays.

Step 2. Lay the months out in order on the floor or on a table so you can see them all at the same time.

Step 3. Mark off the weeks you will take vacation. Yes, this comes first. If you wait until you "have time," you will never have time. Don't know what the kids' school break schedule is? No problem. Use this year's as a guide and adjust it when the new calendar comes out.

Step 4. Mark off the days of each week that you will not work and will focus 100 percent of your time and attention on those you love. Yes, this comes second. Don't give the people you love your leftovers. It works best for everyone involved if these are the same days each week. Spouses, significant others, children, and dogs can take just about anything as long as they have predictable time scheduled with you.

Step 5. Mark off the days of each week you will spend doing support work (i.e., work that has to get done that does not directly generate revenue). Even if you have a support team, you still need to have days when you do your part. Stuff such as: paying bills; planning out the next thirty, sixty, or ninety days; exploring new speaking or writing opportunities; making changes to your blog theme; cleaning off the top of your desk, etc. Yep, you've got to commit at least one day a week to making these tasks your primary focus. It keeps things from catching on fire. You are many things, but a fireman is not one of them.

Step 6. Mark off the days of each week that you will focus solely on the revenue-generating activities of your business. These could be speaking, coaching, writing, holding workshops—whatever it is you DO to earn money. Don't have any revenue-generating activities to schedule? If so, spend these days making sales calls or whatever it is you need to do to get these activities scheduled.

Step 7. Now transfer what you've put together onto whatever calendar system you use most regularly. This is the maintenance piece. There are a lot of electronic methods and apps you can use. Me...I like a paper personal planner.

You now have a rough map to help guide you through the coming year. Of course, it isn't perfect or foolproof (run from anyone who says they have a foolproof system for mapping out your life; they don't). But it does give you something to work with. When you get lost or bogged down and can't seem to find your way, pull out your map. Figure out where you are. Figure out where you want to go. Adjust your compass and head out. A byproduct of mapping out your year is you can build in fun as a reward for the hard work you do. Having a plan and accomplishing goals become a vehicle for motivation to move you forward.

BENEFITS OF EFFECTIVE PLANNING

Together, the baseline for tracking and plotting your weekly schedule and yearly map will reduce your stress, increase your productivity, optimize your time management, and act as positive reinforcement for completed projects on a daily, weekly, monthly, and yearly basis. If you want to be really ambitious, set one major goal for the next few years. Pick a goal for years two through five then a very broad goal for year ten. Record your goals on a 3x5 index card and tape it to the inside of your kitchen spice cabinet. Weird? You'll see the goals on the card every time you open the cabinet to add spices to your cooking. It's kind of symbolic of keeping your life spiced up. Anyway, it feels downright delicious to put a checkmark by completed projects for work and play as the years come and go. Keep yourself flexible when it comes to modifying your long-term goals. Want a little extra positive reinforcement? Share your yearly calendar and your yearly goals with another person. Sharing increases the probability of accomplishing your desired goals.

It is essential for you to decide on what time management system works best for you. I like an old-fashioned paper system like At-A-Glance or Franklin Covey planners. If you are a digital native, a free digital system like Google Calendar, Zoho Calendar, or Cozi Family will work well. There are pros and cons to all systems. Find one that fits you, then commit to using it religiously. As a result of the analysis of your personal energy cycle and mapping a year, you have probably discovered you need a boost to help you undertake many entrepreneurial responsibilities. Building a team is next. I refer to my team as my booster chair. Although I am including many possibilities for building a booster chair, you may want to add a few of your own. Let's take a look at the possibilities.

SUPPORTING ROLES

Merriam-Webster defines "booster" as "an enthusiastic supporter" or an "auxiliary device for increasing force, power, pressure, or effectiveness." When something is boosted, it is lifted up. How can you get boostered? I just made that word up. Who do you want in your corner to be like a booster chair to lift you up and support you?

A solo entrepreneur wears a lot of hats. Hats you may not have heard of before. I don't want to scare you with the long list. I do want you to be fully aware so you can build a booster chair that is comfortable, cost-effective with good value, and beautiful in your eyes, and that promotes physical and psychological well-being. George Meszaros writes on the blog *SuccessHarbor* that successful businesses build teams and systems to help the business function and enable it to grow.[45]

Let's figure out how this works for you. Take Lauren Aycock Anderson's story of launching her private practice, Counseling for Creatives. While she was working her way through college, she was a graphic artist and played in a band. She liked graphic design well enough to design her own logo and marketing materials for her private practice. She also knew a little bit about website design, but it drained her to spend time learning the technology for how to build a great website. Lauren contracted with a web developer to build her website. However, she knew enough about websites to update her own with content for her blog. Lauren liked writing and playing music, so she created and managed her own videos, music, and content on her website. Plus, as a graphic designer she created many of the images. Check her out at *laurenaycockanderson.com*.

Do you have skills you enjoy that you can use in the first phase of your private practice? Are there tasks on the list that you have the skills to do but you dread doing? What will help you soar?

I attended a business school right after graduating from high school. I received good grades and all, but I absolutely dreaded the tedious ledger work. I bet you can guess the first person I hired. You got it, a bookkeeper. I hired her for two hours per month in the beginning. I wasn't busy with a heavy caseload and revenue, so it did not take the bookkeeper much time. Within six months she had a system figured out for the business where she only had to work one hour per month. It was great! It was simple! It was affordable! It was win, win, win. The cool thing about contracting with a service provider like a bookkeeper is you can negotiate how the process will work for you. Count on the fact there is somebody who is willing to sell you their services.

The next person I hired was a web developer, Kevin Turner, owner of *789WebDevelopment.com* and solo entrepreneur. Thanks to the bookkeeper streamlining the bookkeeping process, I could afford to have a web developer help me build a website. *He* did not build the website. That's right; he helped *me* to build my own website, and I loved learning how to do it. Kevin was like a tutor. I did the easy stuff, and he took care of the more technical aspects. I love collaborative processes. Hey, isn't collaboration a therapy skill? Collaboration opens the door for synergy to happen. It's like magic. Keep looking until you find the person who will fit the bill.

The following list includes roles and tasks that may or may not apply to you. It is inclusive of the typical roles and tasks of most small businesses. As you read through it, notice what roles and tasks feel energizing, draining, curious, or neutral. Make a few notes in your journal, or write directly in this book.

Next will be learning how you can find people to give you a boost when you need it. I have used Angie's List and Thumbtack and found local people. With online freelance services, you can hire almost anybody from anywhere in the world. Remember to ask for referrals from your network of family and friends. Some popular sites are Fiverr, Upwork, Guru, Freelancer, and 99Designs.

I have confidence in your ability to build an effective team to boost your endeavors while you focus on building your private practice business.

Supporting Roles

- Accountant/Bookkeeper

- Administrative/Receptionist/Scheduling

- Business Coach (I used a coach for six years)

- Computer Expert

- Website Developer: design and development

- Customer Service

- Decider: asks question about prioritizing the what, when, how, who, why; partner or mastermind

- File Clerk: can be a professional organizer who helps you set up your office

- Financial Analyst: for pricing, client retention, growth; bookkeeper or CPA can perform this function for you

- Human Resource Manager: that's you—who are you going to hire?

- Graphic Designer: business cards, brochures, flyers, logo

- Innovator: creative solutions to obstacles and problems that can be related to the business or service to your clients; coach, mentor, mastermind group

- Mail and shipping: bills, marketing, products—down the road as you grow

- Marketer: this will be you most of the time
  - Networking
    - Groups face-to-face
    - Individual one-on-one

- Social Media Coordinator: It's a big mistake to try and be on too many social media platforms. Your well-designed website with a blog or vlog will serve you well. All other platforms are used to drive clients to your website. Choose one and master it then add a second.

  - Facebook
  - LinkedIn
  - Blog/Vlog
  - Twitter
  - Instagram
  - Google +
  - Pinterest
  - YouTube
  - The next big thing not yet innovated. Alignable was just hitting the internet and quickly growing in the late 2017s

- Social Media Analysis: anything from website traffic (SEO) to conversion rates from online directories. Sometimes the Social Media Coordinator or Website Developer can support the analysis of how well your website is performing along with how well your social media engagement is performing.

- Production Manager/Worker
  - Blog/Vlog
  - Podcasts

- Visionary: projection and forecasting in alignment with strategic business planning; coach, mentor, mastermind group

Private practice business owners who are willing to hire someone grow their practice faster and become more prosperous more quickly with less stress. The four roles that offer the best in stress relief for time and energy are: accounting, writing and social media, graphic design and web development, and administration support.

ACCOUNTING

A reputable accountant will help you stay on top of your taxes, and they can offer you sage advice about business growth and asset protection. Ask around to find a good one. You can contact the American Institute of CPAs or your state chapter of the Society of Certified Public Accountants. Your CPA can recommend a qualified bookkeeper. A bookkeeper's fees are about one-third of what a CPA charges. An added benefit of using a bookkeeper and accountant is the IRS is less likely to audit you since you use a professional who is held to professional ethical standards.

If you prefer doing your own bookkeeping, use a software program that is easy for you, such as Intuit, QuickBooks, or Mint. I use a combination of paper, bookkeeper, and a CPA. I record my revenue on paper in a ledger. I write on each receipt the purpose of the purchase. The categories are minimal: office supplies, marketing, continuing education, etc. My bookkeeper set up an easy system for me to use. Monthly, I add up my revenue, gather my receipts, and send everything to my bookkeeper. At the end of the year, my bookkeeper sends the compiled information to my CPA. My time investment is about one hour per week. The bookkeeper works about one hour per month. The CPA charges by the project. The information the bookkeeper tracks allows me to control my expenses and aids in forecasting business cycles.

WRITING AND SOCIAL MEDIA

If you love writing posts for your blog, keep it up. I learned from my mistakes that I have a blind eye when it comes to proofreading, so I need help with blog writing. You should have an editor or a set of fresh eyes to proofread your writing. You can ask a friend who has good writing skills, or you can hire an editor. An app like Grammarly is good too, and it is free.

If you are writing copy for your marketing materials, such as a brochure or your website specialty pages, hire a professional freelance writer to help you. Nothing is more embarrassing than typos and poor grammar. It is expensive to have marketing materials printed twice because of spelling errors or typos. Bite the bullet and pay upfront for a professional. You can be budget-wise by searching sites like Upwork or Speedlancer. You can also use Fiverr under the category "Writing & Translation." Craigslist is an option too. I have used Thumbtack with mixed results. You can search Google for freelance writers but make it specific, for example: "freelance writer for mental health and anxiety." LinkedIn is yet another option, as is Twitter. Gosh, where would we be without social media platforms? There are plenty of freelance writers and editors out there. Ask for references and ask to see a sample of their work.

Whoever you hire should be able to catch your voice. We all have a unique cadence to our speaking and writing, and your freelance writer needs to be able to capture your authenticity. I am stressing the importance of spending a lot of time on writing, because it is the first connection you will have with your potential clients. Your rapport-building starts when your potential client reads your blog, your bio, or your brochure, so it needs to sound like you. First impressions matter. Be diligent about your hiring and writing processes.

GRAPHIC DESIGN AND WEB DEVELOPMENT

Unless you were a graphic designer or a web developer in your former life, forget the DIY project. I know there are easy-to-use platforms for websites like Wix and Weebly that make building a website as easy as pie. As of this printing Google does not rank these types of platforms in their algorithms. That being said Google changes its algorithms on an unpredictable schedule. The so-called internet spiders and crawlers overlook site-building platforms such as Wix and Weebly, making it harder for your clients to find you. That being said, I get it! You are new at the private practice thing and want some kind of website. I agree. You can get a prefab website from Brighter Vision, TherapySites, or TheraNest until you are ready for a custom-designed website. TheraNest is also a therapist directory. For online directories, have a consistent bio prepared you can use across the internet and include a call to action. A call to action is a phrase telling your potential client what to do next, such as "Call me today."

Be an informed consumer and read about how to build a website or watch a few educational videos on YouTube. The two biggest recommendations I have for you when choosing who and how to build a website are 1) use *WordPress.org* not *WordPress.com* for building your website; 2) self-host it. Almost all web designers and developers can use the *WordPress.org* platform, so if you need to switch contract providers, you have a system everybody knows. I would also recommend Squarespace. It is an easy-to-use platform, and Google crawlers and spiders will rank and index your website.

ADMINISTRATION

Imagine this: You are the CEO of Private Practice Help You, and only you can retain the services of a virtual assistant (VA), or an administrative assistant, to support you. I know it sounds bold to think of yourself as a CEO, but that is exactly the role you are in, and nobody but you can make the important decision of hiring. Don't get stuck in a Superman role and let overwork become the kryptonite of your career. A good match in a virtual assistant is amazing. You can hire a VA by the project at Upwork. Professional organizations like Global Alliance of Virtual Assistants (GAVA) and the International Virtual Assistants Association (IVAA) have directories you can search. A couple of other directories are AssistU and VA Networking.

It can be challenging to find a well-rounded VA who can help with social media postings, writing, bookkeeping, data entry, and so on. A good one who knows the therapy world will be in high demand. They often contract by the month. Before you hire a VA, spend time getting clear on what you want to delegate. When I started, I could not afford a professional VA, so I hired a freelance writer who wanted to break into the field of virtual work as an administrative assistant. Together we designed her job; it was like an internship.

If you think you don't need a VA now or you can't afford one, consider putting it on your wish list for down the road as your business grows. There are virtual assistants who specialize in clerical assistance or technical assistance, and some specialize in creative assistance. The average range in fees for a VA is $20-$80 per hour. If you want to know what to pay for other freelance help, check out the PayScale website at: *www.payscale.com.*

OUTSOURCE OR AUTOMATE

Take notice of the roles and tasks you want to keep for yourself (they are energizing for you). Beyond the obvious role of therapist, is there anything else you want to keep? Next look for the dreaded tasks you want to delegate. Can you contract someone to do the work? Keep in mind you have a limited number of hours in a day, so spend them wisely.

As the architect of your private practice business you are the only one who can choose which features will boost you and your business. But what criteria should you use to make these decisions? To reiterate, it will behoove you in the long run to outsource the tasks that drain your energy and focus. Although money is a factor in the beginning, you can start small and outsource more as you grow. It will save you money in the long run to build a team that will act in a synergetic style.

If you are not in a position to hire or delegate, see if you can automate a task. You can use automated programs and apps to take care of a lot of tasks. Electronic health records (EHR) systems offer features for progress notes, scheduling, and invoicing, as well as reminder calls to clients. You can use an EHR system as a time management tool rather than Google Calendar. Systems like Tame Your Practice and Therapy Notes are designed for mental health practices. You can check out the top-rated programs at Capterra. Any type of automated system you use needs to meet HIPAA (Health Insurance Portability and Accountability Act) compliance standards.[46] Businesses that deal with protected health information (PHI) must have secure physical space, such as a locked office and file cabinets, encrypted internet networks, and security measures in place, and must follow measures to ensure the system meets secure HIPAA compliance standards. Covered entities (anyone providing treatment, payment, and operations in healthcare) and business associates (anyone who has access to patient information and provides support in treatment, payment, or operations) must meet HIPAA compliance.

As I continue to tell you…I am an old-fashioned kind of gal and still use a paper planner and paper files for notes, and I still answer my own phones. Part of the hard work as an entrepreneur is figuring all this out since there is no silver bullet. You will need to whip up your creative juices to find out how you want to focus your skills and on what with the precious 86,400 seconds you have in a day. You want to develop effective patterns of behavior.

SUMMARY

Effective time management begins with an accurate assessment of how you spend your time. You have a natural rhythm in the way you live your life on a daily, weekly, monthly, and yearly basis. How you strategically plan to outsource or automate tasks will influence your ability to enjoy the perks of being a private practice business owner. Effective time management will influence how you provide services, because you will have a greater level of energy and focus for your clients. The biggest benefit is you will have a greater sense of control over your destiny.

The key is to remain flexible and adjust as needed. You have a list of possible supporting roles to boost your productivity and a list of possible automated systems to put in your toolbox. Keep tasks for yourself that you enjoy. Before moving on to Section Five: Launching Your Private Practice, I have a few questions for you to ponder.

1. What will help you move toward what matters most to you personally and professionally?

2. What keeps you from moving toward your goal?

3. If all barriers were removed, what would you choose to do?

4. How would you like things to be?

5. What do you want to do next?

Spend some time percolating on your answers, then write your answers in a journal.

Launching Your Private Practice

Picture yourself walking up a three-story ladder on a high dive. Picture yourself walking to the edge of the diving board. See yourself standing there. Notice what your mind begins to do. It is good at keeping you safe. The hesitation to fling yourself off the high dive is perfectly normal. Do you take the next step? Are you ready to launch your private practice business? Are you ready to take the leap and dive in?

I hear people say they are going to "try" and do something. "Try" is a key word in the previous sentence. How do you "try" to jump off a diving board? There is no trying. Diving is a commitment to do that thing that scares you—jump. Either you do it or you don't. It's that simple. You can prepare for the event (which is what you are doing by reading *Sweet Spot*). You may experience feeling scared and apprehensive, and you may experience feeling brave and determined. You might even find yourself stuck, frozen, at the end of the diving board.

It's OK to choose to turn around and go back down the ladder. Maybe private practice is not your thing. In my heart, I hope you make a choice based on what matters most to you. A choice based on appetitive rather than aversive reasons. However, if you find yourself teetering on the edge of the diving board with a desire to jump, yet with a knot in your stomach, be assured you have what it takes to launch and succeed. In this section you put your skills to use. We are going to put together a plan for your launch, so all you need to do is follow the steps.

Because I care about your success, I emphasize to you the need to bring along a wholehearted *commitment* to taking your time with this last section. In this section are the final steps for your future success. You completed experiential exercises in the previous chapters, providing clarity, so you can take intentional and purposeful action. Why the emphasis on being prepared with a solid plan as a foundation? Research after research article points to one of the main reasons a business fails is lack of good planning and entrepreneurial knowledge.[47]

This section covers finding an office space, decorating and furnishing it, and hosting an open house. You will learn about the importance of project management when it comes to event planning and how marketing fits into effective project (event) management. Money is a big concern when starting out, so I give you a list of budget questions to answer. A therapist's office is often referred to as the container for holding the therapeutic process, both literally and figuratively. We'll start with decorating ideas for your office—call it container magic.

CHAPTER

16

Establishing Your Container Magic

The old real estate maxim is as true as ever for the success of your private practice: location, location, location. As in all real estate transactions, it is best if you know what you are looking for before you go searching. To prepare you to go on an office hunt, let's do a visualization. If you are skeptical about visualizations, bring your curiosity with you to see what shows up.

The act of visualization is a focusing behavior. Visualization is used by sports psychologists to help prep athletes for improved performance. Every little detail of the game is covered, from the moment a person walks down the hall to the locker room to the action in the game. You can benefit in the same way, as you see yourself walking down the hall to a successful private practice. The effective method to complete the visualization is to read it first, then record it so you can listen to the exercise script. Smartphones are great for this. You can also get another person to read it to you. Make it vivid. Make it detailed. Make it today.

Visualize Your Location Exercise

Give yourself approximately ten minutes to complete this exercise.

Get in a relaxed space where you will not be disturbed. Give yourself permission to allow your imagination to roam freely. Allow yourself to be released from the judging and evaluating thoughts of your mind. If a *yeah but* or a *what if* shows up, acknowledge it and let the thought move on as you turn your attention back to your private practice. Allow your mind's eye to see, smell, touch, hear, and taste your visualization with exciting fullness and detail. Allow for symbols and metaphors to enter your awareness. Interpretation and the deeper meaning may emerge later as your visualization sharpens over time. Read through the visualization once, then come back to it. Perhaps you'd like to invite a couple of colleagues to gather and take turns reading the script to each other while you listen.

Success Script

Let your eyes close or find a neutral place to look…Allow yourself to take a few gentle, deep breaths in and out…With each inhale, notice your breath as it enters through your nostrils…notice the temperature of the air…notice the direction of the inhaling breath… notice any scent or smell in the air…With each exhale, notice your belly as your breath leaves your lungs…and exits. Again, notice the temperature and the direction of the air as your breath leaves your body. As you take a couple more breaths, notice any sensations in your body where your body touches the chair or sofa…just notice your body as you become aware and connect with your breath… Again, breathe in deeply…And breathe out completely.

If your mind distracts you, that is what minds do. Just notice your thoughts and bring your attention back to your breath…back to the sensations in your body…back to the sounds in the room… just let yourself notice in the present moment.

Now that you feel present, allow yourself to imagine that it is sometime in the future. A month from now or six months from now or a year from now—it's up to you. This is your opportunity to experience being in your private practice. To start this journey, pour all of yourself into the future as if it is right now…pause…pause… See yourself and experience yourself gently drifting toward your desired reality. Experience yourself filled with a sense of purpose… pause…take a look around as you begin to ready yourself for the beginning of your day…notice what you are wearing…the texture and color of your clothes…you are dressed comfortably for a day at your office. As you head to the office take a look around…Notice your commute to your office…it is not too far and not too close to your home. Take a look around on your commute and notice the smells and the sounds on your way.

You are now arriving at your office and entering the building…Notice what is around you. Look about and take in the environment…breathe it in. The space is pleasant with the colors and textures that resonate with you. Notice the size of the room or rooms, as they are the container for your craft…a container for your calling…take a moment to notice people in the space…clients or colleagues….pause. Notice the smell of your space…pause… pause…pause…What is the energy like?…Pour yourself into awareness of the details…pausing to observe your experience…exciting and thrilling or…serene and grounding…or perhaps inspirational and uplifting? …Take in the details…If you find your mind distracting you, thank it, then turn your attention and focus back to your visualization.

Now go to a specific spot in your work space as you prepare for the day…Perhaps it's a table and chair, a counter, or a seat at a desk or by a computer. Maybe today it's outside in the open air, in the expanse of nature. Visualize wherever it is that you can truly engage with your work. Take in the essence of this specific spot…take a long pause…What is the message that it tells about you and the impact of your private practice?…What is the message it tells of how you run your private practice? Allow yourself to connect with what brings you the most joy and fulfillment in your work…What values are you honoring in your work?…How are they a reflection of what you and your private practice is known for?…Take another long pause…

Allow yourself to be fully present with experiencing your private practice as wildly successful and overflowing with abundance. You are earning money easily and effortlessly doing what you love. You see people willing to pay you again and again for your healing work. What do you notice about prosperity, wealth, and abundance in your private practice as you plan how to spend your earnings?…pause… In addition to your financial success, you have achieved your goals and dreams. What successes and milestones have you celebrated? What awards or recognition have you received? What is new or different in your business this coming year? What new products or services are you offering? How have you grown, expanded, or evolved? Pour yourself into the experience of realizing a fulfilling and meaningful career in private practice…let yourself breathe in feelings of satisfaction, excitement, and hope.

Widen your awareness to your breath in your body as you notice where you are sitting in the room. Bring yourself back to the room where you are now. Notice any sounds. Take a few breaths in and out. When ready, open your eyes. Take a stretch.

Sit with your visualization and let it percolate for a few more minutes, as more details will rise with a few minutes of quiet. Then write in your journal, recording as much detail as you can remember, including images, colors, sensations, and emotions. Below are a few questions to stimulate your writing work. If you find yourself tempted to censor or judge the images that arise, hold the judgments for later. Let it flow.

Reflection Exercise

- What stands out most in your visualization?

- What did you notice about the details of your day?

- What was the drive like? How long and where? Close or far?

- What were you wearing? Top, bottom, shoes?

- What colors, smells, sounds, and textures stand out?

- What did your office look like? Colors, plants, books, desk?

Once you complete the journaling, talk through your visualization with a trusted colleague or friend. To deepen your explorations, have your friend ask you open-ended curious questions about your visualization. You do not need to repeat the visualization or post it anywhere. Keep in in your journal and review your answers as needed. Add to it if you feel called to fine-tune it. Remain open and watch out for shoulding on your dream.

LOCATION, LOCATION, LOCATION

The fun begins when you filter through your visualization to create a wish list to give to a property manager or leasing agent. The information generated from the visualization, the details that emerged from journaling, and the clarity derived from talking with a trusted person provide you with a great starting point for finding a good location with a space to fit your needs. Are you ready to complete a list? How do you find what you are looking for?

Sometimes it's as easy as posting a request on Facebook. Most local real estate companies have people who are leasing agents or can refer you to a leasing agent or property manager. A leasing agent generally works for the owner of the building, so you will need to be on your toes when negotiating a lease agreement. Even if you decide to use connections through social media, you still end up in a position of negotiating a lease agreement. How are your negotiating skills? If they're rusty or you are a novice at negotiating, the best thing you can do is stick with your list, know your budget, and take someone with you before signing. Educate yourself on the average square-foot fee for leasing an office of your ideal size.

This is the first time I have mentioned budget. Whoa. Budget is pretty darn important. I will provide a list of common costs incurred in running a private practice business. I strongly suggest you plug in the numbers for your area.

BUDGET

The costs of doing business can be mitigated by office sharing, subleasing, or starting a part-time private practice, such as a boutique practice. A boutique private practice carries a small case-load and is structured to offer specialized niche-type services catering to a well-defined high-end client. Office sharing is when you and another person split or share costs of the office. Subleasing is when you lease office space in a suite with other therapists sharing a common waiting room, kitchen area, Wi-Fi, copier, and other office equipment. Sometimes the subleased office is furnished and other times it is not. I began my private practice by doing an office share.

Budget is a driving force in structuring your private practice business, and rent is the number one highest recurring expense. The list below is arranged from highest to lowest expense. Some will be zero, and the list is not all-inclusive.

Business Costs

1. Rent
2. Utilities
   a. Phone
   b. Internet
3. Office Supplies
   a. Paper
   b. Pens
   c. Computer ink/toner
   d. Coffee
   e. Tissues
   f. Postage
   g. Magazines or books
4. Marketing and Advertising
   a. Website
   b. Online directories
   c. Business cards/brochures
   d. Electronic health records (EHR) systems
   e. Social media (usually costs time, not money)
5. Supervising/Consulting/Coaching
6. Student Loans Repayment
7. Banking Fees
8. Licenses and Certifications

9. Memberships to Professional Organizations

10. Continuing Education

11. Insurance

12. Networking
    a. Coffee
    b. Meals
    c. Gas

13. Tax Preparation
    a. CPA
    b. Bookkeeper
    c. QuickBooks or other software

14. Miscellaneous
    a. Repairs
    b. Donations
    c. Charge card interest
    d. Savings
    e. Salary
    f. Lawyer
        i. Review paperwork
        ii. Business structure (LLC, PLLC, DBA, sole proprietor, etc.)

15. Start-Up Budget
    a. One-time cost for office furnishings and equipment
    b. Optional website; research options with knowledgeable resource

You might wonder when your private practice business will be profitable. The best thing to do is consult your bookkeeper and your accountant. Tax laws and profits are tricky to figure out. A rule of thumb is most businesses do not turn a profit the first year. Although your private practice business does not reflect an actual corporate profit, it can generate a good level of revenue and reflect what is called a "ramen profit." Ramen profit is when you generate enough revenue to sustain a minimal lifestyle. Consider your financial goals and the stage of your career. A formal corporate profit might not be your goal. I entered private practice as an encore career after completing a longtime stint in Corporate America. An encore career comes toward the latter part of a career life cycle, and it is what I call the sweet spot in my career life, as I love what I do each and every day.

Shall we continue to flesh out details from your visualization?

SURROUNDINGS

Do you want your office to be close or far from home? If your office is close, you most likely will bump into your clients in your community. Ask yourself if you are OK with that. My true story is I chose close to home. I work out at a local warm-water aerobics class, and the facility has only group shower rooms rather than individual shower stalls. After a class I am in the shower, you guessed it, naked with shampoo in my hair and in hops a client for the next water aerobics class. She gets dressed in her swimming suit, and then jumps into the shower next to me before heading off to the pool. We do not make eye contact. The whole scenario felt pretty awkward. It's one thing to bump into a client at the local grocery store and quite another thing in the shower room. If you have children, they may go to the same school as your clients' children. Or if you work with children, your child might be in the same class as your client. There are pros and cons to different distances from home to office. Know what you are comfortable with. Having an office a little farther from home allows you to decompress before engaging in home life, which is a nice transition.

Another factor to consider once you decide on distance is ease of access to highways and streets. Also, leasing in an office building with ample parking, close to public transportation, or on a corner with a traffic light can make the difference in attracting clients. Maybe an office building is too sterile, so you choose to lease in a renovated house. The same concerns about ease of access, parking, proximity to public transportation or even to hospitals and medical buildings apply. They all add up in attracting clients to your practice. As soon as you find a location, you will need to consider your office space. Is it conducive to the population you plan to work with? Notice foot traffic flow, windows, lighting, plants, and noise.

- Foot traffic in the building: Is it too heavy for your clients to feel like their visit to your office is confidential?

- Lighting: Is there plenty of natural light? If you are on a lower floor, is there plenty of room for lamps? You do not want to use overhead fluorescent lighting, as they can feel like interrogation lights.

- Plants: Use live plants only, because they reflect you are caring, and plants bring the healing properties of nature into your space. Definitely no plastic plants (more details are provided in the Designing Powerful Healing section later in this chapter).

- Noise: When you are shopping for your office, be mindful with your five senses and notice noises from outside such as traffic, construction, and airplanes. Notice the noise from the room(s) next to you. You can mitigate some noise problems if the landlord is willing to install soundproofing. What do you see, feel, and smell when in the building or office space? I learned the hard way, as I fell in love with a lovely third-floor corner office. I did not notice it was across from the bathrooms, which sometimes had offensive odors. It had great natural lighting but was next to the elevator shaft too, which echoed into my room. And it was on an easy-access corner with a stoplight.

The problem was that the street had heavy weekday traffic, so during rush hour, siren noise pierced the quiet of the room.

- Length of lease: The longer the lease, the cheaper it is up-front as you build. Negotiate for growth. Also, you can ask for more upgrades such as new paint or carpet when you negotiate a longer lease. Be sure to clarify if office sharing is allowed.

- Amenities: Are other rooms included in the lease, like a lunchroom or conference room? Some buildings offer a small gym and/or a shower area. One of my colleagues had a small swimming pool in her building. I was green with envy, but it was too far from where I wanted to lease.

- Home office: There are pros and cons to all office scenarios. Choosing a home office has unique circumstances to consider. The Zur Institute offers an online course on how to have a home office and takes a critical look at the clinical, personal, and familial complications of boundary challenges unique to providing therapy in your home.[48] The Zur Institue also offers a course they call *TeleMental Health*. With the COVID-19 pandemic in 2020, providing tele-mental health services (virtually through video, phone or email) became the chosen method for providing health care. It is ideal for a home office model of providing care.

- Concierge services: You can offer sessions where the client is—home, office, or walk-'n'-talk in the park—and avoid the office altogether. This is ideal for a boutique practice.

- Decorating: Give thoughtful consideration to colors, pictures, and furniture choice. For example, a leather sofa/chair might be offensive to animal rights advocates. When it comes to decorating, consider that pictures of your family are a form of self-disclosure. I am not saying don't; I am saying think about it. (Decorating is covered in detail in Designing Powerful Healing below.) Be mindful of clutter too.

You know there is no perfect office in the perfect location. Check out the list of a few things you can do when you find your mind in the hamster wheel of analysis paralysis:

- Set a deadline and write it on your calendar

- Share your deadline and talk to an objective, supportive person

- Look at the big picture and skip the small stuff

- Use the process of elimination

- Make a choice and do it

Sign a lease. I forgot to mention quite often the first month's rent is free. Now you are ready to give the space a touch of your personality and create a powerful healing space.

DESIGNING POWERFUL HEALING

What does science tell us about designing an office environment that enhances the therapeutic process? You probably already have a good idea about how you want your space to look and feel. Before the 1970s, spaces in hospitals and beyond, which included the therapist's office, were designed for the function of equipment. Most spaces did not even have air-conditioning. The exceptions were X-ray and radiology spaces, and the only reason those rooms had air-conditioning was for the function of the equipment, which would not work unless kept cool. The term *institutional design* is used to describe the architectural structure, the work-space flow, and interior design. The human factor is left out of the institutional design equation for service providers and consumers.

That all changed when a layperson by the name of Angelica Thieriot was hospitalized in 1975 with a mysterious viral infection that nearly killed her.[49] The same year, her son was hospitalized with osteomyelitis, and her father died after a long stretch of battling cancer. Needless to say, she spent a lot of time in hospitals. Her dreadful experiences as a patient began a revolution, and she coined the term *patient-centered treatment*. Fortunately, the revolution spread to all aspects of healthcare. The zeitgeist of the times was marked with the World Health Organization (WHO) in 1978 as it proposed some basic tenets for healthcare.

Family-centered care (FCC) emerged within the pediatric healthcare community. The pediatric healthcare community developed a philosophy where the family is the expert and equal in a partnership with providers. FCC is founded on a collaborative relationship, with the family having access to health information to make decisions based on their values and cultural needs.[50] No longer were families relegated to the long halls of echoing voices when a member was hospitalized. Fathers no longer waited for the doctor to announce the arrival of their child. You get the picture. Today's delivery or birthing room has no resemblance to that of yesteryear.

With the revolution of person-centered services came the scientific community of researchers looking for answers to guide our choices. More recently, people like Jack L. Nasar, PhD, professor at Ohio State University Knowlton School of Architecture, has written extensively on the interplay between aesthetic design and human behavior. Nasar and Ann Sloan Devlin, PhD, professor of psychology at Connecticut College, conducted a research project on people's perceptions of room decor and counselor competence.

The results indicated two significant factors about perceptions.[51] Neatness and chair comfort ranked high on people evaluating the competence of the counselor. The second tier of design importance was order, space, style, and color. Family photos and personalized items ranked lowest in importance.

The study revealed decorating trends you may want to consider for your office. Examples taken from the research of Nasar and Devlin are covered in the following pages.

PUTTING YOUR SPACE TOGETHER

The first question to ask yourself is, *Is my office inviting and welcoming?* How do you imagine the waiting room? First impressions matter. Evidence-based findings indicate the offices viewed by research participants in Nasar and Devlin's study used words like "comfortable," "nice," "clean," "warm," and "inviting" to describe their favorite office choices. Another major factor was orderliness. Messy, cramped, uncomfortable, and cluttered spaces ranked low.

Creating a space that feels secure and safe is important and should match the population you work with, be it children, teens, families, the elderly, couples, men or women, or people who have a temper. Design studies affirm the powerful impact of natural elements, which add to the feel of an interesting and harmonizing environment with the incorporation of suitable color. I say suitable color, because you may not want to use red with domestic violence clients. Yep, red is not a good choice for angry clients, although red may add a sense of aliveness to the room for a person who is feeling depressed. Soft shades of pink, peach, or floral designs might not be such a great idea if the population you want to work with is male. When making choices about decorating, bring yourself into your design and consider your client's experience. It is clear there is a correlation between the design and the therapeutic relationship. The bottom line based on research strongly suggests you will be judged as less or more competent based on your office decorating style.

Credentials

I already mentioned that you can bring yourself into your decorating and design choices. Let's begin with your credentials—should you or should you not display them? In the beginning phases of my private practice I received a lot of advice from my peers about the dos and don'ts of decorating and whether I should or should not display my credentials. I heard it all. Hanging my credentials was showing off and would alienate my clients and cause a power differential that was nontherapeutic. On the other end, I should display all my training certifications and credentials so as to enhance the client's confidence in me. They would know I am a real therapist and highly qualified. This train of thought included the idea that clients would be more willing to pay me more money for services based on the number of certificates hanging on the wall. Thank heaven for people like Nasar and Devlin who spend time researching this kind of stuff.

Research indicates the ideal number for displaying your qualifications is some place between four and nine, with little difference between the two. So, pick a number between four and nine and hang that number of items on a wall the client can see. What about placing family pictures where your clients can see? Most people in the research conducted by Nasar and Devlin were neutral. My advice is consider your client(s). If you are working with people who are struggling with infertility, consider whether you or don't you want to display pictures of your children. Pictures of family, vacations, and other fun carefree activities might work as encouragement—or just the opposite.

Everything in your office says something about your personality. What message do you want to communicate? Is it helpful? The credo within the healing arts culture is "Cause no harm." Be intentional in your choices and sensitive, as most people seeking therapy are struggling. What is the therapeutic value of the pictures to the clinical relationship? Get clear about the function of your decorating choices.

Furnishings

Next to consider are the larger pieces of furniture in your office. How do you choose your chairs, file cabinet, desk, bookcase, table, and sofa? Tori DeAngelis provides useful insights.[52] When possible, stick with natural grains for wood products such as tables and bookcases and skip the glass and chrome. Balance is the secret in mixing the textures of your furnishings. Incorporating wood into your office decor reduces stress, but if you have too much wood, say over 45 percent of your visible decor, it loses its stress-busting quality. People like the appearance of natural grains but don't want to feel they are in a wood box.

How much money should you spend? Buy nice stuff but not too nice. Most visitors to your office will feel comfortable with middle-range furnishings, and this suits people in a broad socioeconomic range. Both your chair and the client chair should provide support and be comfortable. Your spine health is dependent on a properly ergonomically designed chair. It is wise to spend some extra money on your chair since you will spend a good portion of your time there. Being comfortable and taking care of your spine health will allow you to maintain a present-moment connection to your clients. Clients need to have enough room to shift in their seat. A sofa is optional unless you are working with families and couples—or if you are a Freudian psychoanalyst, which is a whole different decorating scheme.

Arrange your furniture to foster a smooth flow of communication. Coffee tables in the center of the room situated between you and the client are not a good idea, but if you do want one for completing games or other therapeutic tasks, then choose a round table. Consider glass as a coffee table, as glass feels less obstructive. Your files are a special concern for protection of privacy. Regardless of what kind of filing cabinet you use or if you go with an EHR system, you will want to be sure only your eyes have access to the files. Confidentiality is a must for promoting a safe-feeling container.

Accessories

Flowers have the power to either energize or calm. According to Sally Augustin, PhD, applied environmental psychologist and principal at Design With Science, green leafy plants can increase creativity and improve cognitive performance.[53] Even the scent of flowers can have an effect on our mood, so bring cut flowers from home and certainly have a plant or two in your space. A therapist's office is often referred to as the container for holding the therapeutic process, both literally and figuratively. It is where the magic of therapeutic healing happens as the therapist provides a safe and accepting presence with boundaries for the relationship to evolve and grow. Flowers and plants, along with other aspects of nature, can provide a softening to the sharp points in the darkness where we travel with our clients. Fill your container with nature. Plastic plants and plastic flowers don't count. Choose plants that help de-stress your space.

- Aloe Plant

- English Ivy

- Rubber Tree

- Peace Lily

- Snake Plant

- Bamboo Palm

- Philodendron

- Spider Plant

- Red-Edge Dracaena

- Golden Pathos

If you do not have a green thumb or you have hay fever, you can have pictures of nature. Just looking at landscaping has been shown to lower blood pressure. Along with plants or pictures of nature, let the light shine in. Natural light is a mood enhancer. No windows? Use table lamps that promote cozy and comfortable feelings. Make sure the lighting is bright enough to discourage a feeling of romance. You can buy lightbulbs with full-spectrum luminance to copy the sun's natural healing power.

Pillows and small throw covers can add a sense of comfort. A small table placed by the client's chair can lend a feeling of support and security. I like to set a tissue box and a small trash can near the client's area. Have water, tea, or simple snacks in the waiting area. Magazines and coffee-table books also add to the comfort of a waiting room. Use positive distractions in the waiting room. Water, such as a small fountain, an aquarium, or a fishbowl, is considered a positive distraction. I kept a bamboo palm in a glass vase with a beta fish on my desk for years. Wallace J. Nichols, author of *Blue Mind*, presents anecdotal and scientific evidence for the mood-enhancing effects of water. We enter a state of "drift" where we can experience a spiritual connection. It feels like water "meditates you."[54] Small fountains work well and add sound to the environment. Plus, a small water fountain in the waiting room can be a noise barrier for clients.

If you are not sure how to decorate your office, hire a pro. Hire a feng shui decorator for fun or final touches and learn about the five elements of energy and spatial flow based on wood, fire, earth, metal, and water. You can find a consultant through the International Feng Shui Guild. A few online affordable interior decorating services are Decorist and Havenly. You can also use HomeAdvisor and Angie's List for local designers. The bottom line is to create an environment that is welcoming, harmonious, and uncluttered. Decorate with your five senses. What do you and what does your client see, hear, smell, feel, and taste? Yes, taste counts too. Coffee, tea, candy. Sit in each spot and notice with your five senses. Notice your orientation in the space. Your body presence is a sense beyond sight, sound, smell, touch, and taste.

PANDEMIC

Many people quickly adjusted to working from home during the Covid-19 Pandemic. A very quick growth is happening with telehealth. The same discussion goes for building container magic for a home office. Your client will get to peek inside your office. What do you want them to see? Also, consider you are sitting inside the container even though your client is not with you, how you decorate your container is just as important as if your office was located in a different building where clients come to see you. You are in the container. Some clinicians keep an office even if they are providing telehealth. They desire the separation between work and home. You decide what works for you and make it magical!

SUMMARY

We have covered details for creating the best-fitting location and decorating schemes. With all the work, exercises, and reading you have done, you are reaching a point of culmination and celebration of all your hard work. While keeping an eye on your start-up budget, you can fashionably create your sacred container where the magic of therapy takes place. The space establishes opportunities for you to work with your ideal client. Colors, smells, textures, sounds, art, and photos all contribute to your sacred container magic designed for saying this is your place for healing, helping, guiding, and walking with another human being. Once the stage is set, your next big project is an open house. Exciting!

CHAPTER

17

Open House Project Management

One of the high points in a private practice business is the day you officially and publicly state you are accepting clients. Go ahead, try it on. Say it loud and clear: "I am open for business" or "I am accepting new clients." An open house is a ritual where you declare you have arrived at a landmark of significant importance in your professional life. Step into your reality. Claim your spot in the community. Honor yourself. Your hard work and accomplishments call for a celebration. An open house also honors all the people who helped along the way and makes a commitment to stay connected and further develop your professional identity and role in your community.

"Open for business" for a private practice is obviously not the same as open for business selling dresses, pots and pans, trousers, or other commodities. You are in the service industry with a focus on well-being. An open house consecrates your move from one state of being, student or employee, to another state of being, entrepreneur. According to research by Francesca Gino and Michael I. Norton, rituals are important because they add to the feelings of being ready, increasing a sense of control, which results in increased productivity.[55] Rituals alleviate feelings of uncertainty and anxiety.

Once you go through the process of project management for an open house, you will have the basic skills for other future projects, like marketing for workshops, therapy groups, webinars, training videos, and product development. Project management incorporates the principles of SMARTER GROWTH for goal achievement. With the knowledge you have gained by reading *Sweet Spot*, you will launch with confidence in your fidelity to live your passion. You are right where you are supposed to be right now.

In the following pages I give you a 360-degree view of how to complete a project starting with the scope of the project. The scope dictates your timeline, costs, agenda, guest list, and phases of development. I provide a comprehensive checklist for successfully completing your first major project (you may download copy of this from my website). As you read about project management, you will be given specific tasks to complete. Whether you decide to host a small or large open house, the bottom line is that you have the opportunity to strengthen relationships in your community. Keep this in mind. Relationship building is the key to growing your private practice business.

PROJECT MANAGEMENT MODEL

If you are moving your private practice to a new location, the process is the same as your "first" open house. You can also host an annual or biannual open house. You can celebrate a five-year or ten-year anniversary with an open house. Hosting regular open houses gets more fun each year and will grow in popularity. Everybody loves a good party.

A popular project management model, the Quality Triangle, illustrates the constraints project managers oversee. A solid understanding of the constraints allows you to develop a plan to address them in an agile fashion.

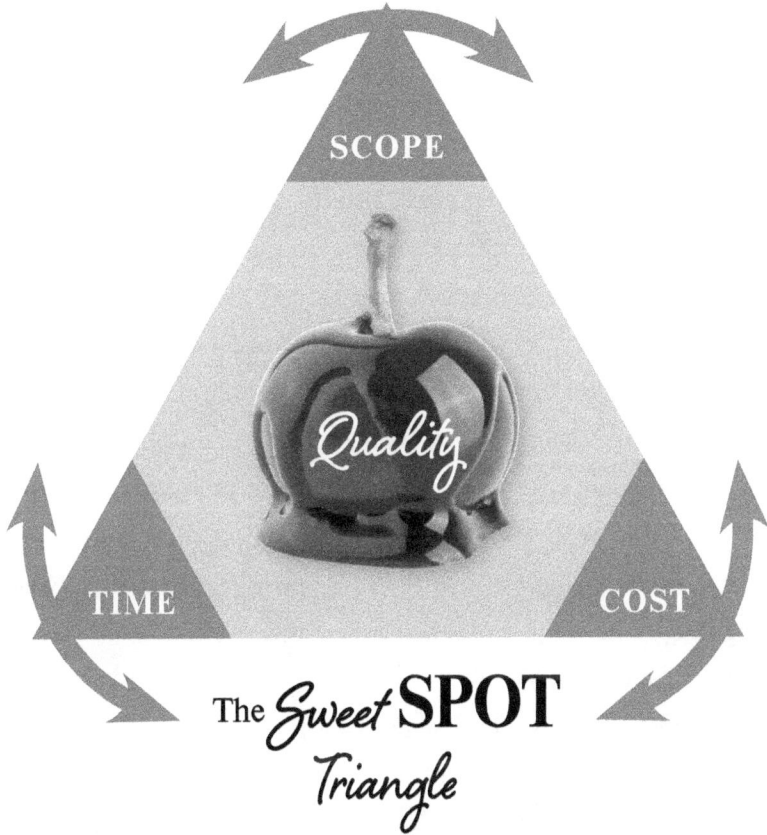

Figure 10: Sweet Spot Project Management Triangle.

Scope

Define your project by first gathering enough information to know how to begin. You need to have a clear idea of the function and goals of an open house. What is your purpose? Is it to bring awareness to your community of the services you offer? Is it to show appreciation to your supporters and allies? Is it to help connect people to each other? In other words, what is the scope of your project? In some ways, defining scope is a lot like formulating a vision and mission statement, because they influence how you communicate, i.e., invitations, theme, and guests.

Schedule

After your research is complete and you have an idea of what you want to accomplish with an open house, you need to ask yourself, *How am I going to accomplish my goal?* You will generate a to-do list that satisfies the schedule function of the Quality Triangle. A timeline is a must for all projects, whether you are planning your open house, forming a therapy group, consultation group, or a mastermind group, or a project such as creating a product to sell or writing a book. Schedule and scope are linked. The Quality Triangle is dynamic; each side changes as you change any one of the others.

Developing and sticking to a schedule seem pretty straightforward. When will you do what? How will you map this out, so you can achieve your goal while meeting your time constraints? I provide a sample timeline for hosting an open house later in the chapter. Other projects might take more or less time than an open house.

Marketing is a big piece of an open house project schedule—or any project as far as that goes. The Rule of Seven, formulated by marketing expert Jeffrey Lant, states it takes seven "touches," or points of contact, before a person is willing to take action. This is a good concept, but it means it will take time, and the important idea is that you need to plan marketing into your schedule.

Cost

How much time and money do you want to or can you spend? We're all on a budget of some sort. And there are the same twenty-four hours in a day for everybody. Be realistic about your available time and money. In setting a budget, you might need to take a few things off your to-do list or substitute items on the list. When I hosted my open house, I switched from ordering catered food to doing the preparation myself. I had more time than money. Soliciting my family and friends helped me stay within my budget (time *and* money).

The central focus of the Quality Triangle is to have the highest-quality results for your project's outcome after allowing for the three constraints of scope, schedule, and cost. Take perfection out of the equation. The model allows for you to do the best you can with what you have. Good enough is the bottom line. The tools from SMARTER GROWTH can be used in conjunction with the Quality Triangle to effectively implement schedule, costs, and scope. The results: a smashing-good open house within your time frame and budget.

When working with the Quality Triangle model for project management, you will want to be aware of conditions that can influence outcome. The two caveats are "scope creep" and "feature creep." As the word "creep" implies, these items cause the project to go off target. Scope creep is defined as going over budget in regard to costs and over time in the schedule by adding more tasks. Feature creep is adding more showcase features. The best way to prevent any kind of creeping is to have a clear and well-defined goal for your open house that is in alignment with your vision and mission and is grounded in your values. My message to you is to get a plan, then work your plan with an ounce of flexibility for tweaking details as needed. An accountability buddy can help.

PROJECT LIFE CYCLE: THE QUALITY TRIANGLE IN ACTION

A project goes through predictable phases. This life cycle may feel similar to other developmental theories you have learned. A team of more than eighty people employed by the nonprofit organization Project Management Institute (PMI) developed a five-phase concept: conception and initiation, definition and planning, launch or execution, performance and control, and project close.[56]

The *Sweet* SPOT *Life Cycle*

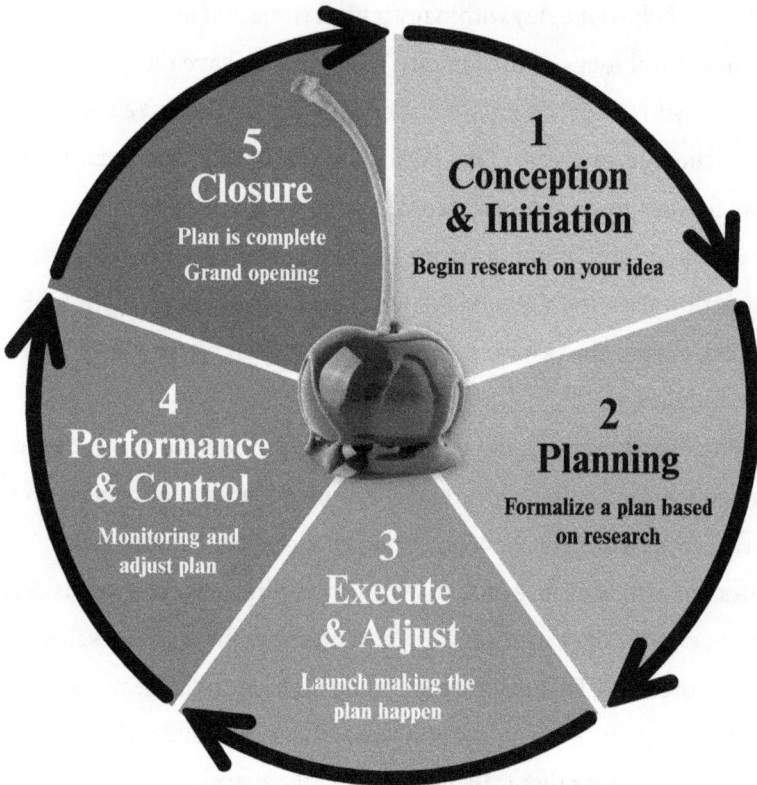

Figure 11: The Sweet Spot Project Management Life Cycle

Phase One: *Conception and Initiation*

I call this phase the "eureka" or "aha" moment. An idea comes to your mind, and it sets in motion the tasks that need to be taken to accomplish a goal. Research is one task and marks the beginning of a project.

I like to approach the conception stage with the end in mind. Maybe you have a concept for a group or a special service you want to offer, like a pre-retirement group for empty nesters. You will follow the same steps and go through the same phases as you do with hosting an open house. With good research you will have a realistic idea of a date to have the project go live—a launch date. Pick a date about three to five months out from your eureka moment. Successful projects need time, and your lovin'. If you have a big idea, ten to twelve months out from the launch date is a good timeline. For the purpose of hosting an open house, give yourself four to five months *from the time you sign a lease.*

I experienced anxiety about hosting my own open house. I gave my fear and anxiety a name like a book title: *Full of Myself.* The backstory behind the title of *Full of Myself* is from the wise words of a friend. Once upon a time a social contact said to me, "You're so full of yourself." It was not a compliment. I told a close friend about my hurt feelings. I'll never forget her lighthearted response: "Who else are you supposed to be full of?" Silly me! Of course, I can be full only of me. I can't be full of someone else. Consequently, when my fear and anxiety tempt me to stay small, I call it the *Full of Myself* story and keep on keeping on.

Share your launch date with someone you trust and who cares about your success. I used my business coach. Also ask someone to help you do some of the leg work. Ask yourself where you need an ally. For me, it was designing the invitation and creating a goody bag for people. Be prepared to confront your biggest fears at each stage with a willingness to have the fears and follow through with committed action.

Phase Two: Definition and Planning

I call this phase the "recipe for success." In this phase you will further define the scope of your project and set a budget based on your research. The planning phase is like spelling out the recipe with ingredients, measurements, and cooking time. Take time to consider the different ingredients you need. Further clarify by writing out your project in a few sentences or a paragraph, articulating the purpose of your event and how to go about fulfilling the purpose.

In this instance, what do you want to accomplish with an open house? We talked earlier about building relationships within your community. What kind of relationships and with whom? What do you want your community to know about you? An open house provides you with the opportunity to talk about your vision and mission and gives you a chance to learn about the passions of other people in your community. Remember reciprocity. What can you offer your community and the individuals in your community? Keep an open mind. Allow your creative self to expand into possibility. Choices abound in Phase Two. Develop a recipe you can follow, with some agility built in.

I suggest you identify a nonprofit that serves your clients and invite the executive director to the open house. When I hosted my open house, I invited members of People House, a nonprofit offering affordable counseling and internships for therapists in training. (I completed my internship at People House.) As with many nonprofit organizations, they are dependent on volunteers and donations. People House was in the middle of a redecorating project and needed paint, pillows, and pictures, as well as snacks and refreshments, for their clients and volunteers. It was easy to ask guests to bring a little something to the open house as a donation for People House. You can provide a list based on the suggestions of the executive director of the identified nonprofit. I am absolutely positive you can identify a nonprofit organization in your community that will benefit from your alliance with them.

Once you have a clear idea of the purpose, you can move to consider another ingredient in the recipe to success: the budget. The Timeline and Checklist below will give you ideas for what you may wish to include in your budget. Remember to be realistic.

One of those budget items is a goody bag. The goody bag can include almost anything. It seems recipes and mindfulness scripts are popular with therapists. Be sure to include your business card in the goody bag. I don't think you have to go to a lot of expense to have a fun goody bag. You can even paint rocks or small pieces of tile with inspirational words or short quotes. As an ACT therapist and coach, I included a script for a defusion exercise along with a finger trap. The script was printed on pretty paper.

Your open house timeline (see an example with a checklist below) will be developed in Phase Two. It is important to write the timeline out and enter it into some form of a scheduler. It is also beneficial to ask your helper if you can assign tasks to them. One task I learned about that makes a lot of sense is to solicit one of your gregarious friends to greet and welcome guests as they show up. A greeter is like a cohost and can help with the guest book, so you can capture contact information and send thank you notes. That same gregarious person can be sure each person receives a goody bag before departing.

Phase Three: Launch or Execution

This stage is self-explanatory. This is a great time to turn to your accountability partner. It is good practice to follow your checklist, and be sure to share it with one another person, such as your chosen greeter. If you find yourself procrastinating, build in a reward and connect back to the values of what it means to you to be in private practice. Name the story or thank your mind. Defusion skills allow you to get back to your vision and mission.

Phase Four: Performance and Control

This stage is easily summed up as the monitoring stage. It's similar to a treatment plan for your project. The objective is to keep track of progress and take action as needed along the way. Along the way refers to darn near every step along the way: creating your plan as well as the process of executing your plan. Keep your eyes open. What might cause you to need to make adjustments? Control sounds heavy-handed but means being aware of progress and adjusting. By being in control, you open the door to agility so you can tweak steps and tasks as required by unknown factors that might arise. All the while you need to be sure scope creep is kept at bay.

Although I am not fond of the word "control," Phase Four is about taking responsibility for your actions in creating outcomes you want for your private practice success. Two years after opening my private practice, I moved to a new location. There was a mass shooting at a local theater in Aurora, Colorado, in July of 2012. My open house was scheduled for August 2012. The community responded with anger and skepticism toward the mental health field because the shooter was seeing a psychologist who did not know or detect the potential danger the shooter represented. Other people in the community expressed gratitude toward crisis clinicians who offered their services for free or at a reduced cost following the shooting. Although I did not make an adjustment to my open house plans, being aware of the shooting sensitized me to public opinion. It was a topic high on people's minds.

The heavy lifting of marketing takes place in Phase Four. I suggest you make an effort to track how you like to market and what works best for you, so you can use your experience in the future. You will be monitoring marketing up until the day of the open house. The day before and the day of your open house will require the most flexibility, as you might need to make more goody bags or order more or less food. You will not know until just before the open house what will actually happen. You will have a good idea of what to expect, but nobody can precisely predict reality.

Phase Five: Project Close

This is the time to send thank you cards and take stock of what you learned. What did you learn about marketing? This includes tracking the results of your efforts. What did you like and what did you not like? Hosting an open house affords you the chance to know yourself. Where did your efforts bring about the most desired results? Ideally, you will be able to assess your strengths at building relationships in your community. What will you fine-tune for your next project?

Remember to congratulate yourself. You did it. Go celebrate and honor your accomplishment of taking a risk!

Below is a defusion perspective-taking exercise called "I Am" for you to try out to help keep you moving while gently holding different perspectives of the self. Complete it now or after you read through the sample checklist.

"I Am" Exercise

Step One: In your journal, write:

I am_____, _____

_____.

Allow yourself six lines. After each *I am* write a description of yourself in the form of an adjective that is a subjective observation. Do not write things like, "I am five and a half feet tall and fifty years old and am wearing a red shirt." Those are objective descriptors. Write, for example: "I am angry, I am shy, I am confused, I am wonderful, I am not a good at marketing." Use one- or two-word phrases to complete each "I am" statement; end each statement with a comma as shown.

How did it go? Next slowly, that's right, slowly, re-read each line beginning with *I am* and notice how you feel as you read the adjectives and phrases.

Step Two: After the comma on each of your statements, mindfully write the following two words: "or not." Make sure you take the time to actually do the writing. You will derive the biggest benefit if you do the exercise, not just read the exercise. Doing this exercise in your mind does not count. If you have to set the book down and go get a pen, I'll wait right here. Keep noticing what comes up when you write the words, "or not." Take a moment to reflect, to be sure you understand.

Step Three: Complete the following while sticking with the skill of being mindfully aware of the process of completing this task. Slowly draw a line through all the words after "I am." Examples:

I am ~~scared, or not~~.

I am ~~a terrible business owner, or not~~.

What's left? *I am.* The defusion process provides space between you and your thoughts, which can be handy in helping you connect to your freedom to make choices and to engage in behaviors that serve you—in this case, pursuing the tasks of being an effective business owner as well as an effective therapist.

TIMELINE AND CHECKLIST

Here is a sample timeline and checklist you may use and modify for an open house, a new product or service launch, a workshop announcement, or a new personnel introduction. (You may download another copy from BookSweetSpot.com.) You can use the checklist as a basic marketing plan for almost any occasion. Shorten it up or extend it. I used it for our annual neighborhood picnic. One thing is for sure: once you complete the checklist, you will have experience with effective marketing skills to grow your private practice.

As mentioned earlier, along the way you will have a chance to notice some of the stories the mind will construct to inhibit your efforts. With mindfulness practice you can gently hold behavior-inhibiting stories and move through the checklist. Have an ally to help you stay accountable or offer support. Maybe you have identified a mentor who might be interested. Remember it takes at least seven touches before someone will take action to RSVP to attend your open house. And remember to use call to action words and phrases. People need to be told what you want them to do.

SAMPLE TIMELINE

Conception and Initiation Phase: The idea of "Aha, I think I want to host an open house." Then begins the research for open house ideas.

Planning Phase: Make an agenda—start with the end in mind. Do you want a special guest? If so, include their name on the invitation list. Could be the mayor or a member of the city council or Chamber of Commerce; many cities and towns have a board for economic development. Guests can be the principal of a school, a pastor of a church, a leader in the community, and so on.

Are you a music therapist or a somatic therapist? You can have a guitarist or a masseuse. Think outside the box and make it as grand or as cozy as you want—your guests and plans will reflect who you are and what you are passionate about. Think about offering memorable gifts, recipes, bookmarkers, ink pens, etc.

Execution Phase: Read over the Sample Checklist completely, then go back and complete it for your open house.

Control Phase: Share your plans and talk with your accountability buddy on a regular basis as you implement the plan daily and/or weekly, making adjustments as needed. Watch for scope or feature creep.

Closing Phase: Send thank you cards. You and your helper can do this together. Then take you and your helper out for a treat. Celebrate!

SAMPLE CHECKLIST

4-5 Months before Open House

Date: _____

Decide on the specifics. An ideal day and time to host an open house is Thursday, early evening. Take note of holidays, school vacations, and other events, such as an annual conference, that will draw attendees away.

Solicit items to raffle from colleagues or nearby businesses. This can be an ongoing process while you move through the timeline. The boxes below are for checking off the list as they're *done*. The yumminess of positive reinforcement is in the checked box:

☐ Date for open house: _____

☐ Time of day: _____

☐ Location—your office: _____

☐ Budget (this might change): _____

- Food: _____

- Beverages: _____

- Goody bags: _____

- Decorations: _____

- Name tags: _____

- Gift cards for any dignitaries: _____

Have a theme or brand. Design for paper invitation cards and online cards. Stick with a theme that matches your brand/image. Keep in mind thank you cards for later, as you can design these at the same time. Invite a VIP guest or speaker. Include VIP guest information on the invitation. Include instructions or special information about parking. Vistaprint or Zazzle are affordable options for your printing needs. If you want to hire a graphic designer, use a freelance online platform to hire one.

Designate helpers. Recruit one or two people who are willing to help and to whom you can delegate tasks.

☐ Helper One: _____

☐ Helper Two: _____

☐ Delegate the these tasks and roles to your helpers:

    ☐ Design and/or send invitations

    ☐ Greeter/host: It's your open house, but your greeter can help people as they arrive

    ☐ Accountability buddy who will keep you on schedule with support

    ☐ Goody bags: What goes into them, preparing them, and handing them out on open house day

    ☐ Thank you cards: Have a matching theme design and have someone address the cards and get them in the mail in a timely manner

3 Months Before Open House

Date: _____

☐ Send invitations and announcement blast. If you do not have enough time to post on all social media platforms, pick the ones you most enjoy. The rabbit hole of social media deserves your cautionary discretion (see Chapter 15 for a list of social media platforms and make a list of possible guests from your Hansel and Gretel Contact Form).

- ☐ Social Media
  - Facebook
    - Your Business Page
    - Groups
    - Your Timeline
  - Eventbrite
  - LinkedIn (activity and blog)
  - Instagram
  - YouTube
  - Twitter
  - Website/Blog
  - Pinterest (great to save images from your blog or vlog post)

- ☐ Community Calendar

- ☐ Event Page on Website

Now that you have an overview, it is time to put the game plan into action. Invite local businesses that might serve your clients. Get permission to post an announcement in your office building.

- ☐ Invite and confirm dignitaries: make it as personal as possible with a printed invitation and a follow-up phone call

- ☐ Email blast to your list if you have Mailchimp, Constant Contact, etc.; otherwise, your personal list

- ☐ Invite property manager or owner of building

- ☐ Paper invitation to other businesses in the building

☐ Allied service providers (see Chapter 14, Who Serves Your Client, and Beyond?): invite them if it fits—fellow students, instructors, family, friends, colleagues

- If your mind tells you that you are a pest, this is a great time to thank your mind and stick with your plan. Create exciting BUZZ

2 Months Before Open House

Date: _____

☐ Finalize any specific orders for food and beverages. You can plan to prepare the food yourself or use a local culinary arts school

☐ Decide on any decorative touches, such as flowers, and order or purchase as needed

☐ Buy and make goody bags. Be sure to include your business card. You can offer a coupon for a complimentary consultation

☐ Post again on social media

☐ Start your RSVP list

1 Month Before Open House

Date: _____

☐ Confirm your special guest will be in attendance and ask if they need anything specific

☐ Firm up the RSVPs and send gentle reminders

☐ Post to social media accounts

☐ Email those in your personal list to remind them to RSVP

☐ Create a sign-in sheet or guest book with address options for email or mail

2 Weeks Before Open House

Date: _____

☐ Repeat above list and let people know there are only two weeks left to RSVP

2-3 Days Before Open House

Date: _____

☐ Clean and prepare your area

☐ Meet with helper(s) to go over all the details. Two or more sets of eyes!

☐ Optional: do a last chance blast on social media accounts to RVSP now

1 Day Before Open House

Date: _____

- ☐ Finish food and drink prep or confirm with caterer

- ☐ Set up office if you have extra tables or chairs

Open House

Open House Day: Set up and be ready early. (Remember this checklist works for other events such as workshops, training, retreats, etc.)

- ☐ Finish setting up

- ☐ Decorate with flowers or other items

- ☐ Check that bathrooms are clean

- ☐ Set up food and beverages

- ☐ Set business cards out

- ☐ Extras: music or videos, classmates' and professors' photos

- ☐ Guest book to be signed as entering or leaving: Greeter can help with this and be sure to give each person a goody bag. Nobody leaves empty-handed

1-3 Days after the Event

Date: _____

☐ Designate helper: _____

☐ Send thank you cards to attendees and guests

☐ Follow up with any questions people had

☐ Post photos on social media

☐ Evaluate event with your helper(s)

How was it? What came up for you as you read over the list? I am excited for you as you arrive at a time and place for launching your private practice business. Can you believe it? You have arrived!

Take time to notice where you were at the beginning of reading *Sweet Spot* and where you are now. Are you finding your groove?

SUMMARY

Although an open house serves different purposes, the bottom line is to develop relationships. First and foremost, the relationships you develop in your community will be the bedrock of your professional life. And an open house is one avenue of affirming your place in the community.

I have structured this chapter so you can gain project management experience, which is one of the many hats a private practice business owner wears. Being a project manager taps into your creative side, which I've paired with a practical step-by-step process. A blueprint is provided that you can modify for any project. With any project, it is important you are clear about the purpose. This chapter is the culmination of the work you have done to find clarity then act on your aspirations.

CONCLUSION

Stop the words now. Open the window in the center of
your chest and let the spirits fly in and out.

—Rumi

Whatever you dream of, it is possible. The biggest obstacle you face is the story your mind tells you about staying safe and not playing with fire.

I live in Colorado part-time, and we experience forest fires that burn thousands of acres to the ground. What comes back does not resemble what was lost to the fire. At first, pioneer plants quickly take hold. The dark canopy of old growth is lost, leaving an opening for sunlight to reach the forest floor and providing conditions for a greater diversity of new plants to thrive. The new forest that replaces the old is called a "second growth" forest. Nature has a way of recovering. Chances are, you are not going to burn down the forest. And even if you do, you, too, have a way of recovering. Open yourself up to the opportunity of letting sunshine reach through the canopy of fear. You have a diversity of ideas waiting to flourish. And the world is waiting for you.

Obviously, a book cannot totally prepare you for being a business owner or magically infuse you with an entrepreneurial spirit. *Sweet Spot* provides a solid foundation. Doing entrepreneurial work will be as unique of an experience as you are. Having a foundation is helpful, but *you* are the doer in your life, and nobody can tell you exactly how you are going to do your private practice. Similar to when we tell clients they are the expert in their lives, you are the expert of how you will imbue your private practice as a business owner, entrepreneur, and therapist with your uniqueness.

When I worked in human resources as a mentor to new employees, Hero Files help set the stage for future success. A Hero File is a folder for keeping track of your successes. It can be a physical folder or and online folder. I prefer paper folders. What goes into a Hero File and why? Life is full of ups and downs. Keeping a record of your accomplishments is a great boost for the downtimes. Complimentary letters, workshop reviews, and thank you cards from peers or clients are great to save in your Hero File. It is easy to forget what we did a year ago, and a Hero File helps us remember. A Hero File is your history of well done so you can keep doing well.

You have arrived. You are at your sweet spot. Your transferable therapy skills will come in handy as a business owner, and the core processes from ACT will serve your psychological flexibility and business agility well. Since entrepreneurship is a creative process, much like therapy is a creative process, you will bring forth your ability to listen, assess, plan, and adapt. Much like launching a rocket to Mars, 10 percent is planning, and 90 percent is tweaking to stay on target. Hence, it is important to know where you are going and have a good plan. Go do it! Find your sweet spot and get into the ACT of entrepreneurship.

ABOUT THE AUTHOR

Brenda M. Bomgardner, LPC, BCC, ACS, is a therapist, coach, and clinical supervisor who brings the core principles of Acceptance and Commitment Therapy (ACT) out of the therapy room into the world of private practice and entrepreneurship as an evidence-based process for creating business success. Founder of Creating Your Beyond, LLC, her mission is to influence the culture of private practice to move toward an integration of therapy skills and business skills. She enjoys facilitating workshops on ACT and entrepreneurship and has written hundreds of blog posts. She lives full time in her RV with her husband traveling the country. The open road is her office. Adventure and new scenery is around every corner. Her memorable adventures include scaling a cliff blindfolded while on a wilderness trip, jumping out of an airplane on a whim, riding an ATV in the beautiful Rocky Mountains, and cruising the sands of the Sonoran Desert. You can hire Brenda for workshops, coaching, and public speaking by visiting *BrendaBomgardner.com* and completing a contact form.

ACKNOWLEDGMENTS

Serendipity is the word that comes to mind as I think about who to thank and why. It is as if fate gave me who I needed for each phase of development. In the process of writing *Sweet Spot*, people came into my life at just the right time. I had no idea what I was getting myself into. Writing a book is a challenge; it became my love-hate relationship, with on-and-off efforts to complete the writing.

First, I want to thank Kathy Baur. It was Kathy who planted the seed in my head about writing a book. You were my mentor and coach as I entered my encore career. You exposed me to Acceptance and Commitment Therapy (ACT). My heart is grateful. This leads me to thank the originators of ACT, Steven Hayes, Kirk Strosahl, and Kelly Wilson. As synchronicity would have it, their 1999 book, *Acceptance and Commitment Therapy*, was donated to People House, my internship site. As I explored the counseling rooms at People House, I discovered a well-worn, slightly dusty ACT book. It came home with me for keeps. I also encountered the skillful delivery of ACT from my supervisor, Paul Zwieg, a retired medical doctor. Paul was my People House internship supervisor for the next two years. I appreciate his wisdom in helping me to experience first-hand the benefits of ACT.

After I began my initial research, along came Kate Heit, a cheerful and interested colleague. She asked me almost every time we talked how the book was coming along. Plus, she was part of the original groups I facilitated for the foundation of *Sweet Spot*. In addition to Kate, I am thankful to each group member who actively participated. Kate, I appreciate the way you helped ignite persistence within me. Once I had some momentum writing, I contacted Lisa Tener to edit several book proposals. When I reached a point of feeling discouraged and ready to give up, Lisa said to me, "Your book needs to be published one way or another." Lisa, your words echoed throughout the entire book writing process. Thank you.

As *Sweet Spot* came into a clear focus, Polly Letofsky arrived on the scene. She became my *how-to* person. With her guidance, I found a fantastic editor, Alexandra O'Connell. She was a passionate linguist from the inside out. Along with Alexandra and Polly, a talented graphic designer became involved, Victoria Wolf. I am appreciative of Victoria's ability to add appealing visual images to *Sweet Spot*. The serendipitous appearance of these people happened *without* knowing at the beginning this would happen. As I have heard many times in life, trust the process.

Before moving on, I want to step back to the very beginning of my work history. My first job as a delicatessen clerk was at a grocery store with a Fortune 500 company. My imagination went wild with the opportunities I could pursue working at a Fortune 500 company. I developed a fulfilling and successful career with heaps of training. Dreams came true. I received hands-on training, classroom training, and further development through a college reimbursement program. I took full advantage of each opportunity for career development. I quickly moved up the corporate ladder. I worked with a lot of marvelous people along the way to becoming a division-level Human Resource Specialist. I worked at the division level for over 17 years and loved it. I am thankful to the generous managers, supervisors, and directors who helped me achieve career success.

After I completed writing the entire manuscript, a light was shined on what I could not see. The light came to me in the way of a collegial friend, Nancy Lee. The light was honest feedback. She helped me see a clear path to being more inclusive in my writing. She helped me see a historical systemic bias within the field of psychology. Specifically, there was no "Golden Years" for people of color and minorities. Neither providers nor patients experienced inclusive services. Nancy graciously brought this inequality to my attention. I feel fortunate our paths crossed at an ACT training. Thank you, Nancy, for holding the light with gracious kindness.

A final thank you to the person who stood with me, watching me go through the mysterious and sometimes torturous process of writing a book. He felt like my shadow. He felt like my rock. He was always there. I adore the way he still introduces me after years of marriage, "This is my *bride*, Brenda." To my life partner, David Bomgardner, may we celebrate this accomplishment together. *Your loving Bride.*

REFERENCES AND
ADDITIONAL RESOURCES

BOOKS

Baumgarten, Howard. *Private Practice Essentials: Business Tools for Mental Health Professionals.* Eau Claire, WI: PESI Publishing and Media, 2017.

Berry, Tim. *Hurdle: The Book on Business Planning: A Step-by-Step Guide to Creating a Thorough, Concrete and Concise Business Plan.* Eugene, OR: Palo Alto Software, Inc., 2004.

Bowen, Murray. *Family Therapy in Clinical Practice.* 1st ed. Lanham, MD: Rowan and Littlefield Publishers, Inc., 1978.

Corbett, Lionel. *The Sacred Cauldron: Psychotherapy as a Spiritual Practice.* Wilmette, IL: Chiron Publications, 2011.

Dahl, Joanne C., Jennifer C. Plumb, Ian Stewart, and Tobias Lundgren. *The Art and Science of Valuing in Psychotherapy: Helping Clients Discover,*

Explore, and Commit to Valued Action Using Acceptance and Commitment Therapy. Oakland, CA: New Harbinger Publications, Inc., 2009.

Diana, David P. *Marketing for the Mental Health Professional: An Innovative Guide for Practitioners.* Hoboken, NJ: John Wiley & Sons, Inc., 2010.

Drucker, Peter F. *Management Challenges of the 21ˢᵗ Century.* New York: HarperCollins Publishers, 1999.

Friedenberg, Jay D., and Gordon W. Silverman. *Cognitive Science: An Introduction to the Study of Mind.* Thousand Oaks, CA: Sage Publishing, 2012.

Gladwell, Malcolm. *Outliers: The Story of Success.* New York: Little, Brown and Company, 2011.

Goleman, Daniel. *Focus: The Hidden Driver of Excellence.* New York: Harper Paperbacks 2015.

Grodzki, Lynn. *Building Your Ideal Private Practice: A Guide for Therapists and Other Healing Professionals.* 2nd ed. New York: W.W. Norton & Company, Inc., 2015.

———. *Twelve Months to Your Ideal Private Practice: A Workbook.* New York: W.W. Norton & Company, Inc., 2003.

Harris, Russ. *ACT Made Simple: An Easy-to-Read Primer on Acceptance and Commitment Therapy.* Oakland, CA: New Harbinger Publications, Inc., 2009.

Hayes, Steven C., Kirk D. Strosahl, and Kelly G. Wilson. *Acceptance and Commitment Therapy: An Experiential Approach to Behavior Change*. New York: The Guilford Press, 1999.

———. *Acceptance and Commitment Therapy: The Process and Practice of Mindful Change*, 2nd ed. New York: The Guilford Press, 2015.

Hayes, Steven C., and Spencer Smith. *Get Out of Your Mind and Into Your Life: The New Acceptance & Commitment Therapy*. Oakland, CA: New Harbinger Publishers, Inc., 2005.

Hill, Napoleon. *The Law of Success in Sixteen Lessons*. Meriden, CT: The Ralston University Press, 1928.

Lant, Jeffrey. *Money Making Marketing: Finding the People Who Need What You're Selling and Making Sure They Buy It*. Cambridge, MA: Jeffrey Lant Associates, Inc., 1995.

Lawless, Linda. *Therapy, Inc.—A Hands-On Guide to Developing, Positioning, and Marketing Your Mental Health Practice in the 1990s*. New York: John Wiley & Sons, Inc., 1997.

Locke, Edwin A., Gary P. Latham, Ken J. Smith, Robert E. Wood, and Albert Bandura. *A Theory of Goal Setting and Task Performance*. Upper Saddle River, NJ: Prentice Hall, 1990.

Loewenberg, Lauri. *Dream On It: Unlock Your Dreams, Change Your Life*. New York: St. Martin's Press, 2011.

Nichols, Wallace J. *Blue Mind: The Surprising Science that Shows How*

Being Near, In, On or Under Water Can Make You Happier, Healthier, More Connected and Better at What You Do. New York: Little Brown and Company, 2014.

Pepper, Stephen. *World Hypotheses: Prolegomena to Systematic Philosophy and a Complete Survey of Metaphysics.* Los Angeles: University of California Press, 1942.

Pink, Daniel H. *To Sell Is Human: The Surprising Truth About Moving Others.* New York: Penguin Group, 2012.

Port, Michael. *Book Yourself Solid: The Fastest, Easiest, and Most Reliable System for Getting More Clients Than You Can Handle Even if You Hate Marketing and Selling.* 3rd ed. Hoboken, NJ: John Wiley & Sons, Inc., 2018.

Prochaska, James O., John C. Norcross, and Carlo C. DiClemente. *Changing for Good: A Revolutionary Six-Stage Program for Overcoming Bad Habits and Moving Your Life Positively Forward.* New York: HarperCollins Publishers, 1994.

Truffo, Casey. *Be a Wealthy Therapist: Finally, You Can Make a Living While Making a Difference.* St Peters, MO: MP Press, 2007.

Ziglar, Zig. *Raising Positive Kids in a Negative World.* New York: Ballantine Books, 1986.

———. *See You at the Top.* Gretna, LA: Pelican Publishing Company, 1975.

JOURNAL OR WEB ARTICLES AND PAPERS

Abaho, Ernest, Christopher Kusemererwa, and Richard Akisimire. "Entrepreneurial Success: Do Owner's Entrepreneurial Attributes and Resource Productivity Matter?" *International Journal of Economics, Commerce and Management* (United Kingdom) 11, no. 6 (2014): 1-15, http://ijecm.co.uk/wp-content/uploads/2014/06/267.pdf.

"Alliances." *Entrepreneur.* Accessed September 28, 2018. https://www.entrepreneur.com/encyclopedia/alliances.

Andruss, Paula. "The Five Traits You Need to Dominate Any Industry." *Entrepreneur.* February 5, 2014. https://www.entrepreneur.com/article/229731.

Arons, Bernard S, Richard G Frank, Howard H Goldman, Thomas G McGuire, and Sharman Stephens, "Mental Health and Substance Abuse Coverage Under Health Reform," *Health Affairs* 13, no. 1 (1994).

Augustin, Sally. "The Mental Health Benefits of Flowers." *Huffington Post.* April 1, 2013, huffingtonpost.com/sally-augustin/health-benefits-flowers_b_2992014.html.

Bacon, Jonathan. "How Brands Are Helping to Remove the Stigma of Mental Illness." *Marketing Week.* May 12, 2016. https://www.marketingweek.com/2016/05/12/how-brands-are-helping-to-remove-the-stigma-of-mental-illness/.

Bascom, William R. "Four Functions of Folklore." *The Journal of American Folklore* 67, no. 266 (October-December 1954): 333-349, doi: 10.2307/536411.

Bellwood, Lucy, and Sarah Mirk. "What Does Wonder Woman Actually Represent?" *The Nib*. May 29, 2017. https://thenib.com/ what-does-wonder-woman-actually-represent.

Bithoney, Bill. "Behavioral Health: A Market Ripe for Growth and Consolidation." *BDO*. March 2015. https://www.bdo.com/insights/ industries/healthcare/behavioral-health-a-market-ripe-for-growth#st-hash.92wdsf6u.dpuf.

Brink, Susan. "Mental Health Now Covered Under ACA, But Not for Everyone." *U.S. News* online, April 29, 2014. http://www.usnews.com/news/articles/2014/04/29/ mental-health-now-covered-under-aca-but-not-for-everyone.

Conejo, Francisco, Madhavan Parthasarathy, and Ben Wooliscroft. "On Using Big Five Facets for Entrepreneurship's Personality Research: Conscientiousness' Taxonomy." *Journal of International Marketing Strategy* 3, no. 1 (Summer 2015): 55-74, http://mtmi.us/jims/img/conejo.pdf.

DeAngelis, Tori. "Healing by Design." *American Psychological Association* 48, no. 3 (March 2017): 56, https://www.apa.org/monitor/2017/03/ healing-design.

Dear, Brian. "Optimizing Your Therapy Session Pricing." *iCouch*. January 30, 2017. https://simple.icouch.me/blog/ optimizing-your-therapy-session-pricing.

De Groot, Juliana. "What Is HIPPAA Compliance?" *DigitalGuardian. com*. September 25, 2018. https://digitalguardian.com/blog/ what-hipaa-compliance.

Ferguson, Tom. "Self-Care: Planetree: The Homey Hospital." *Healthy. net*. Accessed October 1, 2018. www.healthy.net/Health/Article/ Planetree_The_Homey_Hospital/1036.

Gino, Francesca, and Michael I. Norton. "Why Rituals Work." *Scientific American*. May 14, 2013. https://www.scientificamerican.com/article/ why-rituals-work/.

Gollwitzer, Peter M., "Implementation Intention: Strong Effects of Simple Plans." *American Psychologist* 54, no. 7 (1999): 493-503.

Gonsalves, Gabriel. "The 4 Pillars of a Conscious Heart-Centered Business." *Gabriel's Blog*. January 18, 2016. https://www.heartintelligence-coach.com/the-4-pillars/.

Goodbaum, Beth. "Overcome Distractions: 6 Concentration Tips." ThomasNet.com, May 10, 2011, https://www.thomasnet.com/insights/ imt/2011/05/10/overcome-distractions-6-concentration-tips/.

Heilman, Kenneth M. "Possible Brain Mechanisms of Creativity," *Archives of Clinical Neuropsychology* 31, no. 4 (June 2016): 285–296, https://doi. org/10.1093/arclin/acw009.

Kaiser Family Foundation. "Timeline: History of Health Reform in the U.S." March 2011, https://www.kff.org/health-reform/timeline/ history-of-health-reform-efforts-in-the-united-states/.

Kuo, Dennis Z., Amy J. Houtrow, Polly Arango, Karen A. Kuhlthau, Jeffrey M. Simmons, and John M. Neff. "Family-Centered Care: Current Applications and Future Directions in Pediatric Health Care." *Maternal and Child Health Journal* 16, no. 2 (2012): 297-305, https://www.ncbi.nlm. nih.gov/pmc/articles/PMC3262132/.

Lapowsky, Issie. "The Entrepreneurial Superhero." *Inc.* November 24, 2010. https://www.inc.com/staff-blog/the-entrepreneurial-superhero.html.

Lavinsky, Dave. "4 Reasons Business Plans Fail." *AllBusiness.com.* Accessed April 15, 2019. https://www.allbusiness.com/4-reasons-business-plans-fail-12523-1.html.

Edwin A. Locke et al., *A Theory of Goal Setting and Task Performance* (Upper Saddle River, NJ: Prentice Hall, 1990).

Logan, Peter Melville. "On Culture: Edward. B. Tylor's *Primitive Culture,* 1871," *BRANCH: Britain, Representation and Nineteenth-Century History.* Edited by Dino Franco Felluga. Accessed November 25, 2018, http://www. branchcollective.org/?ps_articles=peter-logan-on-culture-edward-b-ty-lors-primitive-culture-1871.

Meszaros, George. "What Percentage of Businesses Fail—the Real Number." *SuccessHarbor* (blog). August 15, 2017. http://www.successhar-bor.com/percentage-businesses-fail-09092015/.

Nasar, Jack, and Ann Sloan Devlin. "Impressions of Psychotherapists' Offices." *Journal of Counseling Psychology* 58, no. 3 (2011): 310-20, https://www.researchgate.net/ publication/51158334_Impressions_of_Psychotherapists%27_Offices.

"The New Superheroes: 30 Entrepreneurs Reveal the Superhero Powers They Desire Most in Business." *YFS Magazine.com.* November 15, 2011.

http://yfsmagazine.com/2011/11/15/the-new-superheroes-30-entrepre-neurs-reveal-the-superhero-powers-they-desire-most-in-business/.

Nguyen, Steve. "Grow Coaching Model: A Fascinating Backstory." *Workplace Psychology*. April 9, 2018.. https://workplacepsychology.net/2018/04/09/grow-coaching-model-the-fascinating-backstory/.

Parry, Wynne. "Holy Therapist! 5 Signs Batman May Be Mental." *LiveScience.com*. June 28, 2012. http://www.livescience.com/21267-count-down-batman-diagnosis.html.

Rick, Scott, Cynthia Cryder, and George Loewenstein. "Tightwads and Spendthrifts." *Journal of Consumer Research* 34, no. 6 (2008): 767-782, http://www.sjdm.org/dmidi/Tightwad-Spendthrift_Scale.html.

Rouse, Margaret. "Pareto Principle." *WhatIs.com*. Updated August 2013, http://whatis.techtarget.com/definition/Pareto-principle.

Somma, Gary. "Project Management from the Middle." Paper presented at PMI Global Congress 2008—North America, Denver, CO. Newtown Square, PA: Project Management Institute.

S, Surbhi. "Differences Between Motivation and Inspiration," *Key Differences.com*. April 8, 2016. https://keydifferences.com/difference-be-tween-motivation-and-inspiration.html.

Tuckman, Bruce W. "Developmental Sequence in Small Groups." *Psychological Bulletin* 63, no. 6 (1965): 384–399.

van Mulukom, Valerie. "This is the secret to creativity, according to

science," World Economic Forum, January 8, 2018, https://www.weforum.
org/agenda/2018/01/this-is-the-secret-to-creativity-according-to-science.

Willis, Janine, and Alexander Todorov. "First Impressions: Making Up
Your Mind after a 100-Ms Exposure to a Face." *Psychological Science* 17, no.
7 (2006): 592-598, doi: https://doi.org/10.1111/j.1467-9280.2006.01750.x.

PROFESSIONAL ORGANIZATIONS

- American Counseling Association: *counseling.org*
- American Mental Health Counselors Association: *amhca.org/home*
- American Psychological Association: *apa.org*
- International Coach Federation: *coachfederation.org*
- National Association of Social Workers: *socialworkers.org*

WEBSITES

Association for Contextual Behavioral Science (ACBS): a worldwide
online learning and research community, and a living resource for anyone
interested in ACT, RFT (Relational Frame Theory), and Contextual
Behavioral Science. Many free resources. Membership is available for a
value-based fee. *contextualscience.org*

Chamber of Commerce: local branches countrywide for this business-to-business (B2B) organization. If you plan on serving other businesses, such as offering workshops, training, or team-building programs,
it might be worth considering paying the fee to join. *chamberofcommerce.
com/chambers*

Mind Tools: offers a wealth of organizational information for leadership
and career development. The majority of the content is grounded in the

field of psychology. There is free information and a paid membership. *mindtools.com*

Office of Small Business Development Centers (SBDC): part of the SBA, with countrywide offices. The OSBDC provides free business consulting and low-cost training services, including business planning, lending assistance, and a variety of other resources. The meetings are hosted by leading universities and state economic development agencies. *sba.gov/tools/local-assistance/sbdc*

Passion for Business: provides content for small business owners through coaching, consulting, and mastermind groups. The content is applicable for private practitioners. *passionforbusiness.com/index.htm*

Pickslyde Consulting: aimed at bringing evidence-based practices into the work environment to bring about change in the tone and tempo of an organization's climate. Free resource page with audio recordings, white papers, publications, and other material. *pickslyde.com/free-library*

Portland Psychotherapy: a clinic and research and training center with a unique business model that funds scientific research. There are free ACT exercises on audio files along with other resources. *portlandpsychotherapy-clinic.com*

The Practice Institute: has educational information for the private practice entrepreneur through free resources and paid membership. It is also a press. *thepracticeinstitute.com*

Practice of the Practice: information about monthly revenue in real life, based on the founder and owner's experiences. The content is for beginners and seasoned private practice business owners. *practiceofthepractice.com*

Private Practice From the Inside Out: offers business, marketing, and ethics for private practice business owners with an interest in blogging. *tamarasuttle.com*

SCORE: a completely free, countrywide network of business mentors and a partner with SBA. These mentors volunteer to work with small business owners to help them develop and grow business plans. *score.org*

Small Business Administration (SBA): a government organization that guarantees affordable business loans and other resources for entrepreneurs. Has state and local branches countrywide. *sba.gov*

Therapeutic Writing Institute. Kay Adams: Provides training for therapists, coaches, healers, and anyone interested in self-improvement. *twinstitute.net*

Working With ACT: translates the latest evidence from behavioral science, mindfulness, and ACT into the workplace. *workingwithact.com*

Zur Institute: an educational website for mental health professionals. It offers continuing education credits, certificates, and private practice courses. *zurinstitute.com*

Note: Most websites have a newsletter or blog you can subscribe to. Authors of books often have a website along with a newsletter. Professional organizations provide newsletters too. Almost all the above resources can also be found on Facebook.

ENDNOTES

1   James O. Prochaska, John C. Norcross, and Carlo C. DiClemente, *Changing for Good: A Revolutionary Six-Stage Program for Overcoming Bad Habits and Moving Your Life Positively Forward* (New York: HarperCollins Publishers, 1994), 110-111.

2   Peter F. Drucker, *Management Challenges of the 21st Century* (New York: HarperCollins Publishers, 1999), 168.

3   Mike Morrison, "Write SMART Objectives & Goals – Criteria," *RapidBi.com*, February 5, 2016, https://rapidbi.com/writesmartobjectives/#SMARTERhistory.

4   Steve Nguyen, "GROW Coaching Model: A Fascinating Backstory," *Workplace Psychology*, April 9, 2018, https://workplacepsychology.net/2018/04/09/grow-coaching-model-the-fascinating-backstory/.

5   Zig Ziglar, *See You at the Top* (Gretna, LA: Pelican Publishing Company, 1975), 199.

6 Greater Good Science Center and Berkeley Arts and Letters, "Daniel Goleman on Focus: The Hidden Driver of Excellence," *Greater Good* online, accessed September 10, 2019, https://ggsc.berkeley.edu/what_we_do/event/daniel_goleman_on_focus_the_hidden_driver_of_excellence.

7 Minnesota Council on Developmental Disabilities, "Moral and Ethical Issues Specific to Developmental Disabilities," Minnesota Department of Administration, October 2009: 16, https://mn.gov/mnddc/honoring-choices/cnnReports/Moral_and_Ethical_Issues-Kappel.pdf.

8 Lynn Grodzki, *Building Your Ideal Private Practice: A Guide for Therapists and Other Healing Professionals*, 2nd ed. (New York: W.W. Norton & Company, Inc., 2015), 37.

9 Bernard S Arons, et al., "Mental Health and Substance Abuse Coverage Under Health Reform," *Health Affairs* 13 (Spring 1994), https://www.healthaffairs.org/doi/full/10.1377/hlthaff.13.1.192.

10 Susan Brink, "Mental Health Now Covered Under ACA, But Not for Everyone," *U.S. News* online, April 29, 2014, http://www.usnews.com/news/articles/2014/04/29/mental-health-now-covered-under-aca-but-not-for-everyone.

11 Steven C. Hayes et al. *Acceptance and Commitment Therapy: The Process and Practice of Mindful Change*, 2nd ed. (New York: The Guilford Press, 2015), 330-331. Used with permission.

12 Bruce W. Tuckman, "Developmental Sequence in Small Groups," *Psychological Bulletin* 63, no. 6 (1965): 384–399.

13 Russ Harris, ACT Made Simple: An Easy-to-Read Primer on Acceptance and Commitment Therapy (Oakland, CA: New Harbinger Publications, 2009), 109-110.

14 Steven Hayes, "About ACT," ContextualScience.org, accessed September 10, 2019, https://contextualscience.org/about_act.

15 Zig Ziglar, Raising Positive Kids in a Negative World (New York: Ballantine Books, 1986), 60.

16 Surbhi S, "Differences Between Motivation and Inspiration," Key Differences.com, April 8, 2016, https://keydifferences.com/difference-between-motivation-and-inspiration.html.

17 Maya Angelou quote, published on PassItOn.com, accessed November 20, 2018, https://www.passiton.com/inspirational-quotes/7383-my-mission-in-life-is-not-merely-to-survive.

18 Gabriel Gonsalves, "The 4 Pillars of a Conscious Heart-Centered Business," January 18, 2016, https://www.gabrielgonsalves.com/the-4-pillars/.

19 Credits for contributions to this material include: Lois M. Frey, UVM Extension, RR #4, Box 2298, Montpelier, VT 05602, (802) 223-2389, email: lfrey@sover.net, https://www.uvm.edu/crs/resources/nerl/group/a/a.html, http://crs.uvm.edu/gopher/nerl/personal/growth/b.html, http://www.uvm.edu/crs/.

20 Valerie van Mulukom, "This is the secret to creativity, according to science," World Economic Forum, January 8, 2018, https://www.

weforum.org/agenda/2018/01/this-is-the-secret-to-creativity-accord-ing-to-science; Kenneth M Heilman, "Possible Brain Mechanisms of Creativity," Archives of Clinical Neuropsychology 31, no. 4 (June 2016): 285–296, https://doi.org/10.1093/arclin/acw009.

21 Jay D. Friedenberg and Gordon W. Silverman, Cognitive Science: An Introduction to the Study of Mind (Thousand Oaks, CA: Sage Publishing, 2012), 223-227.

22 Lauri Quinn Loewenberg, Dream On It: Unlock Your Dreams, Change Your Life (New York: St. Martin's Press, 2011), 2.

23 Joel A. Barker quote, published on BrainyQuote.com, accessed November 25, 2018, https://www.brainyquote.com/quotes/joel_a_barker_158200.

24 Alison Barr, "An Investigation into the Extent to which Psychological Wounds Inspire Counsellors and Psychotherapists to Become Wounded Healers, the Significance of These Wounds on their Career Choice, the Causes of These Wounds and the Overall Significance of Demographic Factors," (presentation, 3rd COSCA Research Dialogue, Stirling, Scotland, November 9, 2006).

25 Peter Melville Logan, "On Culture: Edward. B. Tylor's Primitive Culture, 1871," BRANCH: Britain, Representation and Nineteenth-Century History, ed. Dino Franco Felluga, accessed November 25, 2018, http://www.branchcollective.org/?ps_articles=peter-lo-gan-on-culture-edward-b-tylors-primitive-culture-1871.

26 Wynne Parry, "Holy Therapist! 5 Signs Batman May Be Mental,"

LiveScience.com, June 28, 2012, http://www.livescience.
com/21267-countdown-batman-diagnosis.html.

27   Lucy Bellwood and Sarah Mirk, "What Does Wonder Woman
Actually Represent?" The Nib, May 29, 2017, https://thenib.com/
what-does-wonder-woman-actually-represent.

28   Marco Caliendo and Alexander Kritikos, "Is Entrepreneurial Success
Predictable? An Ex-Ante Analysis of the Character-Based Approach,"
KYKLOS 61, no. 2 (2008): 209, https://www.researchgate.net/publi-
cation/4993946_Is_Entrepreneurial_Success_Predictable_An_
Ex-Ante_Analysis_of_the_Character-Based_Approach.

29   Jonathan Bacon, "How Brands Are Helping to Remove
the Stigma of Mental Illness," Marketing Week, May 12,
2016, https://www.marketingweek.com/2016/05/12/
how-brands-are-helping-to-remove-the-stigma-of-mental-illness/.

30   Daniel H. Pink, To Sell Is Human: The Surprising Truth About Moving
Others (New York: Penguin Group, 2012), 65-92.

31   Francisco Conejo et. al. "On Using Big Five Facets for
Entrepreneurship's Personality Research: Conscientiousness'
Taxonomy," Journal of International Marketing Strategy 3, no. 1
(Summer 2015): 57, http://mtmi.us/jims/img/conejo.pdf.

32   Janine Willis and Alexander Todorov, "First Impressions:
Making Up Your Mind after a 100-Ms Exposure to a Face,"
Psychological Science 17, no. 7 (2006): 596, doi: https://doi.
org/10.1111/j.1467-9280.2006.01750.x.

33 Stephen Pepper, World Hypotheses: Prolegomena to Systematic Philosophy and a Complete Survey of Metaphysics (Los Angeles: University of California Press, 1942)<<specific pages?.

34 John Elflein, "Any Mental Illness in the Past Year Among U.S. Adults by Age and Gender as of 2018," Statista.com, last edited September 20, 2019, https://www.statista.com/statistics/252311/mental-illness-in-the-past-year-among-us-adults-by-age-and-gender/.

35 John Elflein, "Major Depressive Episode in the Past Year Among U.S. Adults by Age and Gender 2018," Statista.com, last edited August 29, 2019, https://www.statista.com/statistics/252312/major-depressive-episode-among-us-adults-by-age-and-gender/.

36 Bill Bithoney, "Behavioral Health: A Market Ripe for Growth and Consolidation," BDO, March 2015, https://www.bdo.com/insights/industries/healthcare/behavioral-health-a-market-ripe-for-growth#sthash.92wdsf6u.dpuf.

37 Brian Dear, "Optimizing Your Therapy Session Pricing," *iCouch*, January 30, 2017, https://simple.icouch.me/blog/optimizing-your-therapy-session-pricing.

38 Ibid.

39 Margaret Rouse, "Pareto Principle," *WhatIs.com*, last updated August 2013, http://whatis.techtarget.com/definition/Pareto-principle.

40 Ibid.

41 Jonathan B. Spira and Joshua B. Feintuch, "The Cost of Not Paying Attention: How Interruptions Impact Knowledge Worker Productivity," Basex, Inc., September 2005, http://iorgforum. org/wp-content/uploads/2011/06/CostOfNotPayingAttention. BasexReport.pdf

42 National Center for Complementary and Integrative Health, "Complementary, Alternative, or Integrative Health: What's in a Name?" National Institute of Health, updated July 2018, https://nccih. nih.gov/health/integrative-health.

43 Ibid.

44 "Alliances," *Entrepreneur.com*, accessed September 28, 2018, https:// www.entrepreneur.com/encyclopedia/alliances.

45 George Meszaros, "What Percentage of Businesses Fail—The Real Number," *SuccessHarbor* (blog), August 15, 2017, http://www. successharbor.com/percentage-businesses-fail-09092015/.

46 Juliana De Groot, "What Is HIPAA Compliance?" *DigitalGuardian. com*, September 25, 2018, https://digitalguardian.com/blog/ what-hipaa-compliance.

47 Dave Lavinsky, "4 Reasons Business Plans Fail," *AllBusiness.com*, accessed April 15, 2019, https://www.allbusiness.com/4-reasons-busi-ness-plans-fail-12523-1.html.

48 Ofer Zur and Nola Nordmarken, *Home Office* online course, Zur Institute, accessed December 20, 2018, http://www.zurinstitute.com/

homeofficecourse.html.

49 Tom Ferguson, "Self-Care: Planetree: The Homey Hospital," *Healthy. net*, accessed October 1, 2018, http://www.healthy.net/Health/Article/ Planetree_The_Homey_Hospital/1036.

50 Dennis Z. Kuo et al, "Family-Centered Care: Current Applications and Future Directions in Pediatric Health Care," *Maternal and Child Health Journal* 16, no. 2 (2012): 297-305, https://www.ncbi.nlm.nih. gov/pmc/articles/PMC3262132/.

51 Jack L. Nasar and Ann Sloan Devlin, "Impressions of Psychotherapists' Offices," *Journal of Counseling Psychology* 58, no. 3 (2011): 314, https://www.researchgate.net/ publication/51158334_Impressions_of_Psychotherapists%27_Offices.

52 Tori DeAngelis, "Healing by Design," *American Psychological Association*, March 2017, http://www.apa.org/monitor/2017/03/heal-ing-design.aspx.

53 Sally Augustin, "The Mental Health Benefits of Flowers," *Huffington Post*, April 1, 2013, huffingtonpost.com/sally-augustin/health-bene-fits-flowers_b_2992014.html.

54 Wallace J. Nichols, *Blue Mind: The Surprising Science that Shows How Being Near, In, On or Under Water Can Make You Happier, Healthier, More Connected and Better at What You Do* (New York: Little Brown and Company, 2014), 215.

55 Francesca Gino and Michael I. Norton, "Why Rituals Work," *Scientific*

American, May 14, 2013, https://www.scientificamerican.com/article/why-rituals-work/.

56 Gary Somma, "Project Management from the Middle,"
Paper presented at PMI Global Congress 2008—North
America, Denver, CO. Newtown Square, PA: Project
Management Institute. https://www.pmi.org/learning/library/
project-management-middle-five-stages-6969.

www.ingramcontent.com/pod-product-compliance
Lightning Source LLC
Chambersburg PA
CBHW021759190326
41518CB00007B/365